A History of Indian River County

"a sense of place"

Sidney P. Johnston

D1071286

Published by Indian River County Historical Society
2636 14th Avenue, Vero Beach, Florida 32961

ISBN 1-881470-07-5

Printed in the United States of America.

Introduction

The observance in the year 2000 of the seventy-fifth anniversary of Indian River County's organization as Florida's sixty-sixth county inspired the Indian River County Historical Society to publish this commemorative history. The Society chose Sidney Johnston and William R. Adams to perform the historical research for the volume and to put their findings to words. As research historians and consultants for the firm of Historic Property Associates, Inc., in St. Augustine, the two had since 1988 participated in several surveys of historic resources within the county, commissioned by the Society. Consequently, Sidney and Bill had gathered a large base of information and personal knowledge about the county's history long before setting to work on this book.

Many others contributed to it. The Society is deeply indebted to the Schumann Foundation for its support. It made this book possible. For more than three quarters of a century, the Schumann family published the *Vero Beach Press-Journal,* fondly known by long-time residents as the "PJ." Throughout those years, the paper provided Vero Beach and Indian River County with consistently fine reporting. The authors of this book, like many members of the Indian River County Historical Society, have relied upon the newspaper's archives for much of their research material. Its columns and illustrations offer a dependable and deep resource of information about Indian River County.

The Indian River County Historical Society provided editorial and research assistance and guidance throughout the project. Donald Bercaw, Alma Lee Loy, Ruth Stanbridge, and, especially, Judy Owens-Voyles patiently spent countless hours pouring over drafts, photographs, and maps. Most of the photographs and sidebars were drawn from the Society's archives, including manuscript material, photographs, and recorded interviews.

George Keyes and Aline Westfahl at Sebastian River Area Historical Society, Pamela Hall at Indian River County Main Library, and I at the Indian River Citrus Museum provided helpful advice and resource materials. Staff members at county courthouses and school board offices in Fort Pierce, Titusville, and Vero Beach were helpful in locating information at those repositories.

Dr. Gene Lyon, a charter member and honorary director of the Society, graciously made available to the authors several unpublished manuscripts that treat the early history of the area, especially the events that immediately followed the Spanish landing at St. Augustine in 1565. Before Dr. Lyon began publishing the results of his path-finding research a quarter century ago, few students of Florida history realized the significance of this part of the central east Florida coast in the permanent settlement of the state. Without his research, the story would have remained largely untold.

We hope that the people of Indian River County who have lived here a long time will find much in this book that will resonate in their experience; and that visitors and readers afar will find it a fitting introduction to a wonderful land that many of us are privileged to call home.

Ruth Stanbridge
County Historian
October 2000

Dedication

Community Building in Pocahontas Park, Vero Beach, Florida V 19

The Indian River County Historical Society is deeply indebted to the Schumann Foundation for providing the Society the opportunity to publish this book.

For four generations, the Schumann Family has witnessed and recorded many of the events described in the following pages.

It is with sincere appreciation that we dedicate

THE HISTORY OF INDIAN RIVER COUNTY:
"a sense of place"
to the Schumann Family

Contents

IDEAL SUBDIVISION FOR A FORTY-ACRE TRACT IN INDIAN RIVER FARMS AT VERO, FLORIDA.

Chapter One
The First Three Centuries

Carved out of St. Lucie County in 1925, Indian River County was one of thirteen counties established during Florida's last episode of county subdivision. The county embraces 539 square miles of land and water within its boundaries, situated midway on the Florida peninsula along the Atlantic coast. The county took its name from the lagoon that extends southward along the east coast of Florida from New Smyrna Beach to Stuart. Most settlement and development within the county has occurred along the coastline. Wetlands cover a large part of its interior parts. Blue Cypress Lake in the western part of the county is the largest fresh water lake in Indian River County, measuring three by six miles. The wetlands, which provide the headwaters for the St. Johns River, have historically served as a natural barrier to development of western interior spaces.

A relatively few incorporated communities contain the important governmental, educational, and commercial facilities in the county. Beginning at the north end of the county and running along the coast, the major cities include Sebastian, Orchid, Indian River Shores, and Vero Beach, the county seat. Fellsmere is located ten miles inland in the north-central portion of the county. Among the prominent unincorporated settlements are Roseland, Wabasso, Gifford, Winter Beach and Oslo. Interstate 95, U.S. Highway 1, and State Road A1A run north-south through the county. The major east-west thoroughfares, State Road 60 and County Road 510, and three secondary routes, county roads 505, 507, and 512, link the larger communities with Interstate 95. The Florida Turnpike touches a portion of the county, but has no interchange connecting with a county road. The Florida East Coast Railway is the sole provider of rail transportation.

Human settlement of the Florida peninsula began about 13,000 years ago. During the earliest distinctly identified period of occupation, called the Paleo-Indian Era, the inhabitants practiced a relatively nomadic lifestyle, subsisting as

First published in Frankfurt, Germany in 1591, the drawings of Jacques Le Moyne, an artist who accompanied the French expedition to Florida in 1564, provide the earliest known graphic depictions of the aboriginal populations in what is now the United States.

hunters and gatherers. Climactic changes after about 9,000 B.C. permitted the Indians a more sedentary lifestyle. Archaeologists have delineated the beginnings of a new culture, the Early Archaic, as early as 7,500 B.C., when inhabitants from the peninsular central highlands began annual treks to the coast to fish, hunt, and gather shellfish and plant foods. By the end of the Late Archaic period, around 500 B.C., the Indians had developed distinctive pottery types that enable archaeologists today to define individual cultures.

Indian River County is located at what appears to have been a cultural crossroads, archaeologically defined near the Circum-Glades, East-Central, and Okeechobee Basin aboriginal cultures. Evidence indicates that the region served as a transitional area of cultural territories. The Apalachee, Timucua, Tocobaga, and other smaller tribes in the north were mainly farmers who cultivated corn, squash, beans, and other crops that formed the mainstay of their diet, which was supplemented by edible wild plants and animals, in particular deer, fish, and game birds. The southern tribes—the Tequesta, Ais, Jeaga, and others—lived a semi-nomadic existence, relying on gathering seasonal plants, harvesting shellfish, and hunting wild game. A possible exception to the norm in south Florida were the Calusa, who appear to have undertaken some farming in the Lake Okeechobee Basin and on the southwestern coast of the peninsula.

Ais settlements were clustered along the Indian River, its inlets to the sea, and the fresh water creeks and rivers that flow into it. In decades of excavation, archaeologists have discovered many middens (ancient refuse mounds) at locations such as Roseland, Sebastian, Gifford, Wabasso, and Vero Beach. Their investigations have identified major town sites near and south of the present Sebastian Inlet, on both sides of the river. Although the Spanish called the local aboriginal inhabitants primitive and barbarous, anthropological evidence suggests that the Indians here had developed a religious and governmental structure of some complexity. They held long ceremonial dances, maintained separate burial areas, and exchanged goods and captives over an inter-tribal network that extended throughout the southern Florida peninsula. Unlike the Indians to the north of them, principally the Timucua, who inhabited the St. Johns River valley, the Ais did not practice agriculture, but hunted large and small game and, of course, harvested sea food from the waterways along which they invariably lived.

In the half century that followed the announced discovery of Florida in 1513 by the Spanish Governor of Puerto Rico, Juan Ponce de Léon, the Ais Indians experienced frequent contact with Europeans. Frequent offshore shipwrecks delivered European prisoners and salvaged goods to the Indians, provoking trouble. By the time the Spanish established a permanent settlement at St. Augustine in 1565, the Ais had developed a reputation among the Europeans as cruel and fierce warriors. In 1546, a Spanish ship sailing from Panama foundered near Cape Canaveral. The Indians killed its owner and 120 survivors of the shipwreck, but spared the life of a Basque boy named Pedro de Bustinçury. He grew up among the tribe, learned the native language and married the sister of the chief, or cacique. Through meticulous research in Spanish archival records, historian Eugene Lyon traced the eventful life of de Bustinçury, who later visited the French and Spanish courts and still later returned to Florida as a translator for the Spanish colonists.

The man for whom de Bustinçury served as translator, Admiral Pedro Menéndez de Avilés, was sent by King Philip II of Spain in 1565 to establish a colony on

Pedro Menéndez de Avilés led the expedition of soldiers from Spain that in 1565 established the colony at St. Augustine, resulting in the oldest continuing settlement in what is now the United States. Although his historical reputation in Florida is most closely associated with St. Augustine, Menéndez also explored the east coast of Florida as far south as present-day Indian River County. There he sought information about his son, believed to have been lost at sea in that vicinity.

Archaeology in Indian River County

Archaeological investigations along the Indian River actually began in the 1850s, before the Civil War. Concern about survival of the rich underground heritage grew in the late part of the century when road builders began wholesale removal of archaeological sites, harvesting them for the earth and shell they contained. Treasure hunters also mutilated the mounds. In June 1892, D.C. Ervin reported one such desecration in Orchid, where "fragments of skull and other bones, left scattered around, show it to be the burial place of an extinct and peculiar race." Several months later the Smithsonian Institution photographed the site, but little additional investigation along the Indian River took place following the work of noted Philadelphia archaeologist Clarence B. Moore in the 1890s. In assembling a chapter on Florida aboriginals and historic period archaeology for the Smithsonian Institution's *Handbook of American Indians* in 1903, ethnologist James Moody found the "available information relating to the ancient tribes of Florida and the Gulf States...deficient and confused."

Dredging operations often unearthed bones and antiquities hidden in the muck for centuries. An exciting discovery occurred at Vero in 1915, when E.H. Sellards, state geologist, was called in after a dredge unearthed human remains. The site stood at the north edge of town, about one mile north of the depot and one-and-one-half miles west of the Indian River. Intrigued with the find, Sellards requested the assistance of the Smithsonian Institution, which sent physical anthropologist Ales Hrdlicka to the site. Sellards believed the remains belonged to early man. Hrdlicka disagreed, concluding in October 1916 that the Vero finds were most likely of recent origin, associated with the Seminole occupation. The peninsula also yielded promising artifacts. Working in a mound across from Vero, Isaac Weills in 1914 catalogued items for the Florida Geological Survey.

the northeastern coast of the territory the Spanish called La Florida. The king intended to thwart French or English attempts to occupy the strategically important area. As orders for the expedition were being drawn up, word came that a French settlement, called Fort Caroline, had been established near present-day Jacksonville. Menéndez was ordered to destroy the outpost. He landed men and material to establish a settlement at St. Augustine and immediately set off to destroy the upstart French colony. A naval battle between French and Spanish fleets in the waters off Fort Caroline on September 4, 1565, proved inconclusive, but Menéndez led an overland attack on the stronghold, overwhelming its defenders and killing nearly all of them. The French flotilla sailed away, perhaps hoping to attack St. Augustine, but a strong windstorm that lashed the Florida coast a few days later drove the fleet farther south. The ships foundered and the survivors washed ashore along the coast, some as far south as Cape Canaveral. Menéndez hurried south from Fort Caroline. At an inlet twenty-six miles south of St. Augustine that is now called Matanzas (meaning "slaughter"), the Spaniards found and dispatched the first group of survivors. Menéndez and his men continued southward to the Cape, where they found the remaining survivors. The Frenchmen had constructed an earthen fortification protected by cannon salvaged from one of the ships. After a brief skirmish, they surrendered to Menéndez.

Having destroyed the fortification and remnants of the French presence at the Cape, the Menéndez expedition trekked to the narrow isthmus that separates the Indian River from the Atlantic Ocean, where the Spaniards encountered a network of Ais Indian villages. At the place where they found the Indians, the barrier island consisted of a narrow spit of sand, a location now judged to have been near the Sebastian Inlet. Why the Admiral led his force so far south of St. Augustine is questionable, but he may have held hope of finding his son, Juan Menéndez, who had been lost at sea two years before, perhaps off the coast of central Florida, when a hurricane struck his ship. The Admiral parlayed with the Ais chieftain, but apparently learned nothing about the fate of his son.

In desperate need of supplies for both the St. Augustine settlement and his force at the Indian River, Menéndez sailed in search of assistance to Havana on one of the small boats that had accompanied his expedition. He left behind a detachment of 200 Spanish troops and some 50 French captives under the command of his local lieutenant, Juan Vélez de Medrano, warning him to "treat the Indians well." But the garrison's rations soon ran out. Unable to procure food from the Indians, the force under Vélez de Medrano mutinied. About half of their number headed southward, perhaps reaching as far as present-day Stuart. The remainder, loyal to Vélez, proceeded aboard the remaining boat to Jupiter Inlet, where they found a promising harbor and an elevated location. There the Spaniards erected a temporary stronghold, which bore the name Fort Santa Lucía. Vélez soon reunited with the mutineers. The troops remained at the Indian River location until the following February, occasionally trading with the Indians, but more often fighting with them. Thus ended the first attempt by Europeans to settle the Indian River area, now sown with seeds of conflict. Arguments over trade, food supply, and women continued thereafter to exacerbate troubles between the two peoples.

Three years later, in 1568, another lieutenant of Menéndez, Esteban de las Alas, returned to the Indian River with de Bustinçury as translator. At the Indian town of Pentoya, possibly near the location of present-day Palm Bay, the Spaniards gave gifts to the Indians and negotiated "treaties" of amity and cooperation. Evidently, those efforts failed, for in 1573 Menéndez, in Madrid, informed the king that he had made peace three times with the coastal Indians and that they had broken it each time. He listed five Spanish ships that had recently washed ashore on the middle east coast. The Indians, he reported, had captured or killed nearly all of the survivors. So troublesome was the situation that Menéndez asked the king's permission to capture the coastal Indians and sell them into slavery in

The salvaging and plunder of ships wrecked off the coast of Florida became a virtual industry within the communities of Indians who inhabited Florida's east coast. The goods the Indians retrieved and the contacts they made with shipwreck victims threatened the native culture. As the hills in the background reveal, the Dutch artist of this imaginary depiction of such an event obviously knew nothing about the geography of Florida.

the West Indian islands. His request was denied, but relations with the Indians remained strained.

His successor as governor of colonial Florida, Pedro Menéndez Márquez, in 1582 dispatched an emissary to the Ais to barter for the return of five Spanish captives. As translated by historian Eugene Lyon, the governor's instructions to his emissary read: "Arriving at the port of Ais, put yourself in the launch and anchor in the widest part of the river, where the arrows cannot reach you. With the interpreter, tell the cacique from the launch that you give him for me a yard of red cloth, a hatchet, a knife and sheath as a free present; treat him with food so that he feels secure; (obtain the release of the captives), and persuade the cacique that from now on, if some ship wrecks on the coast, that he will send the escaped Christians to this fort with an Indian who will return with the goods in exchange for his safety. If possible, bring a principal Indian to St. Augustine of his own free will; later, I will send him by land very much honored. Keep the soldiers from arguing about trade, and by no means permit anyone to go ashore."

In 1597, the newly appointed governor of Florida, Gonzalo Méndez de Canzo, stopped for water on the Ais coast while sailing from Havana to St. Augustine. He held a friendly meeting with the cacique and decided that, once he reached St. Augustine, he would send an emissary from the capital to negotiate with the Indians. The governor chose an experienced soldier and translator, Juan Ramírez de Contreras, for the mission. The unfortunate emissary and the two Christian Indians who accompanied him were slain by the Ais. The grief stricken widow of Ramírez cried, "they drink from his skull." An enraged Governor Méndez de Canzo sent a punishing expedition to burn Indian towns, initiating a war that lasted several years and did not end until his successor made peace.

Throughout the seventeenth century, an uneasy and often violent relationship persisted between the Spanish and the Ais. The Indians fiercely maintained their independence, prohibiting the Spanish from establishing a fort, mission or settlement in their area. Remarkably, the natives also managed to preserve their basic

Dr. Eugene Lyon

Published in 1976, Dr. Eugene Lyon's historical masterpiece, *The Enterprise of Florida: Pedro Menéndez de Avilés and the Spanish Conquest of 1565-1568,* provided the definitive account of the royal decision to plant a colony in Florida and the events that attended the Menéndez expedition. Eugene Lyon, a long-time resident of Indian River County, served for a time as the city manager of Vero Beach before entering the academic fold. He devoted his career to retrieving from public and private archives throughout Spain copies of documents relating to the colonization of Florida, transcribing many of them, and in his own writings shedding vast new light on the complex early history of the peninsula. Scholars of Florida's early history will remain forever in his debt.

culture, despite the access to goods and technology, such as firearms, that contact with the European afforded them. At times, Spanish soldiers and captains were able to engage the Indians in trade. The Europeans especially sought the precious metals the Indians often salvaged from shipwrecked vessels. A governor of Havana and former official in St. Augustine, Pedro de Valdés, had copper plates fashioned for the Indian trade bearing symbols the natives revered. More often, the two sides fought. In the opinion of historian Eugene Lyon, the Spaniards never truly accepted the Indians' refusal to change their way of life.

Perhaps the most remarkable account of the Ais culture in its waning years was provided by Jonathan Dickinson, a Philadelphia Quaker who survived a shipwreck off the coast at Jupiter in 1696. Dickinson and his family made their way ashore and for a time lived among the Ais in what is now Indian River County, three leagues north of the inlet, before beginning a northward journey upon the beach to St. Augustine. Dickinson kept a day-to-day journal of his trek up the coast in which he recorded his observations of the Indians, about whom he wrote: "These people neither sow nor plant any manner of thing whatsoever, nor care for anything but what the barren sand produce; fish they have as plenty as they please." They collected palm berries, coco plums, and sea-grapes, which they stored for times of want and were reluctant to share. He described a lengthy ceremony that went on for three days and told about the great esteem the Indians held for their chief. The house of the cacique, or chief, wrote Dickinson, "was about forty foot long, and twenty-five foot wide, and covered with palmetto leaves both top and sides. There was a range of cabins, or a barbeque on one side and two ends. At the entering on one side in the house a passage was made of benches on each side leading to the cabins. On these benches sat the chief Indians, and at the upper end of the cabin was the Caseekey seated."

Except for a brief interlude of the British rule (1763-1784), Florida remained until 1821 under nominal Spanish authority. During that long period, Spain made no attempt to create a settlement in the Indian River region or, for that matter, the rest of *La Florida*. Except for mission sites scattered throughout the southeastern continent, ranging at various times from Chesapeake to Louisiana, the Spanish confined themselves to the colonial presidio of St. Augustine. Even there they were soon threatened. Once the English had secured their colonization of the Carolinas in the late seventeenth century, they began to wage a campaign of systematic destruction upon the Spanish mission outposts and the capital itself. In 1702 they burned all of St. Augustine, except for its newly created, massive stone fortress, the Castillo de San Marcos. By 1740, when General James Oglethorpe, the governor of England's newest American colony, Georgia, failed in a further attempt to expel the Spanish from St. Augustine, nothing remained of the missions or of the Indians who had once populated them. Smallpox and measles, diseases the Europeans introduced, had wreaked a fatal toll on the native population. Fewer than 200 Indians remained in south Florida by 1750. European colonizers had completely destroyed the unique and complex cultural fabric of Florida's first peoples.

England finally won control of Spain's Florida colony in 1763, one of the fruits of its victory over France and Spain in the Seven Years War (1756-1763). More than 3,000 Spanish colonists abandoned the colony when the English took over, leaving few inhabitants. The paucity of settlers made it difficult for the British

A map of the east Florida coast, prepared in 1770 by William Gerard de Brahm, surveyor general for the British colonial government, failed to show an inlet within present-day Indian River County. The closest opening to the sea that de Brahm recorded was the Jupiter Inlet, still present in the constantly changing coastline. De Brahm called it the Grenville Inlet. The Hillsborough Inlet seen on de Brahm's map was probably located immediately south of what is today Melbourne Beach. It no longer exists. Some modern scholars believe, despite De Brahm's findings, that the coast along what is now Indian River County did contain a natural inlet at the time.

crown to develop its new colony. Among the efforts made to encourage immigration of new colonists was the Proclamation of 1763, which offered easy terms by which settlers could gain land grants. Articles in journals such as the *London Gazette* reported the ease with which persons willing to relocate to Florida could acquire extensive tracts of rich agricultural land. The new colonial governor, James Grant, extolled Florida's supposedly healthy climate and its potential for making prosperous those ambitious and energetic persons establishing plantations in the colony.

The British divided Florida into two colonies, East and West, making them the 14th and 15th American colonies, respectively. East Florida, its capital at St. Augustine, ran westward to the Apalachicola River. Pensacola became the capital of West Florida, which stretched west from the Apalachicola River to the Mississippi River. The English-speaking settlers who answered the call to occupy the new colony were mainly upper class whites who had resided in Georgia, South Carolina, England, and Scotland. Although thousands of acres were awarded to colonists and absentee investors in the form of land grants, development in the Indian River region was limited to a few temporary plantations.

The revolt by Britain's long-established North American colonies in 1776 threatened the security of Great Britain's two Florida colonies, delaying further settlement and leaving the area vulnerable to attacks by pirates or American rebel forces. The subjects of the crown in Florida were not sympathetic to the separationist aims of their cousins to the north and remained loyal to the king. Three times American insurgents invaded East Florida during the war but failed to capture St. Augustine. Spain, eager to recover its losses of twenty years earlier, seized Pensacola in May, 1781.

The Treaty of Paris, signed on September 3, 1783, recognized the independence of the thirteen former colonies and acknowledged the new nation's boundaries as extending west to the Mississippi River, north to Canada, and south to the Florida. Through the treaty, Spain regained control of East and West Florida. This time, the Spanish attempted to encourage settlement, as the British had, by attracting immigrants with promises of land grants and by permitting non-Catholics to settle in Florida. An oath of allegiance to the Spanish Crown and a promise to convert to Catholicism constituted the only prerequisite for land ownership by persons with the financial resources to establish a farm or plantation.

Enfeebled by war and domestic turmoil in Europe, Spain found itself incapable of governing its Florida colonies, made unruly and chaotic by the border chaos that gripped the post-revolutionary southeastern part of the continent. Homeless Indians, escaped slaves, British arms merchants, and American militiamen crossed the border into Florida with impunity, creating unrest that Spain could not, or would not, control. Oaths of loyalty to the Spanish Crown notwithstanding, settlers from Alabama, Georgia, and South Carolina agitated to bring Florida within the Union. Established planters in the areas of the Halifax, Tomoka, and Indian rivers became increasingly alarmed by the growing violence. One planter in the Halifax area claimed that by 1811, all his neighbors had abandoned their plantations and homes. Spain's uneasy grip on its Florida colonies became manifest when American forces under Andrew Jackson marched unopposed through West Florida and seized Pensacola in 1818. A year later, the Spanish bowed to the inevitable and signed away Florida to the United States. Andrew Jackson returned in 1821, this time as provisional governor of the Territory of Florida. In July of the same year, Jackson created St. Johns and Escambia Counties, the first two political subdivisions of the newly-formed territory. St. Johns County initially comprised all of Florida east of the Suwannee River, including what was to become Indian River County.

The acquisition of the Floridas gave the United States control over a vast and largely undeveloped area ripe for settlement and helped to resolve some of its long-standing problems in the region. Under Spanish rule, the peninsula had provided a haven for runaway slaves and refugee Indians. For more than a century the Creeks and related tribes had drifted into Florida, forced by aggressive white settlers from their ancestral homes in Alabama, Georgia, and the Carolinas. The Indians who sought refuge in Florida united under a new tribal designation, the Seminoles, an English language corruption of the Spanish word *Cimarron*, or "runaway." Numbering an estimated 5,000 in 1821, they were joined by fugitive slaves who intermarried with them or lived in separate villages under friendly relations with the Indians. Once Florida became a U.S. territory, however, American settlers agitated for removal of the Indians. The former slaves who lived among them and who had gained their liberty under Spanish rule faced the threat of re-enslavement.

Changing County Names

Upon taking charge of the new Territory of Florida in 1821, Governor Andrew Jackson created two counties governing his jurisdiction. St. Johns County embraced all of the peninsula east of the Suwannee River. For the next century, Florida continued to be subdivided into increasingly smaller county jurisdictions, ending with 67 counties in 1925.

Two counties whose names have disappeared, Mosquito and Santa Lucia, once governed activities in present-day Indian River County. The name Mosquito County stuck until 1845, when the Legislature discarded it as discouraging to new settlement. Santa Lucia County, organized in 1844, took its name from the temporary fort that the Spaniards set up near Jupiter Inlet in 1565. It was swallowed by Brevard County in 1855 and resurrected as St. Lucie County in 1905. St. Lucie, the matron saint of Syracuse, Italy, inspired the name.

In all, Indian River County fell within five earlier county jurisdictions: St. Johns County (1821-1824); Mosquito County (1824-1844); Santa Lucia County (1844-1855); Brevard County (1855-1905); and St. Lucie County (1905-1925).

New settlers poured into Florida. A change in attitude toward the settlement of the peninsular interior, including the area that became Fort Pierce, accompanied the change of flags. Land speculators and settlers sought their fortunes in the sparsely populated territory, causing real estate speculation to intensify during the 1820s. Despite lack of roads, the absence of ports, and the small number of navigable rivers—plus the constant threat of diseases such as yellow fever—newcomers eagerly sought to establish a foothold in the region. The first territorial census in 1825 revealed that there were still only about 5,000 permanent residents in all of East Florida and but a handful in the Indian River country.

Some plantations had already emerged along the Indian River, engaged mainly in the cultivation of oranges. The Spanish had very early introduced citrus to Florida, planting the trees at mission sites and near St. Augustine. They even exported some fruit to Cuba and other Spanish colonies. Planters during the British Period expanded the commercial exploitation of citrus. Despite the political chaos of the Second Spanish Period, cultivation and export of oranges continued. Groves could be found along the St. Johns River as far north as Cowford, the original settlement of Jacksonville. A killer frost that struck in 1835 on the eve of a devastating Indian war set the industry back several decades or more.

In the 1820s, the Indian River area became part of Mosquito County, which extended roughly from today's Crescent Beach, near St. Augustine, south to West Palm Beach, west to Sebring and north to Ocala. Another important agricultural enterprise along coastal Mosquito County was the growing of sugarcane, which required low bottom lands and access to navigable waterways. The cane was subsequently processed into crystal sugar and syrup. Sugarcane juice provided the essential ingredient in the manufacture of rum, a profitable commodity at the time. Approximately twenty sugar plantations could be found along the coast of Mosquito County in the 1820s. Because sugar production required backbreaking toil, the industry depended on slave labor. By 1830, there were over 500 black bondsmen in Mosquito County. Most planters owned between thirty and sixty slaves. The agricultural development and era of prosperity that much of Middle Florida enjoyed during the 1820s would, however, be cut short in the 1830s when increasing hostility between white settlers and Seminole Indians erupted into the Second Seminole War (1835-1842).

Memories of the First Seminole War (1817-1819) were still fresh on both sides. That initial conflict, which resulted in the temporary American occupation of Spanish West Florida, hastened Spain's abandonment of its Florida colonies

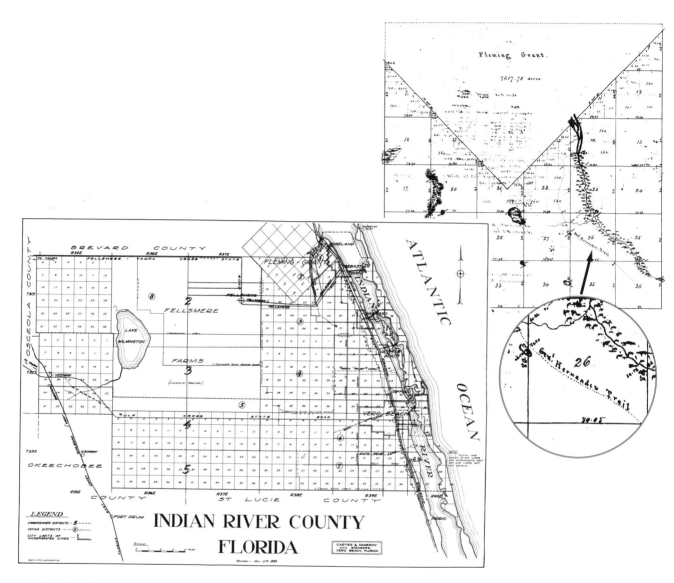

For his loyalty to Spanish authority as a militia officer during the so-called
"Patriot's War," an abortive attempt in 1812 to annex East Florida to the United
States, George Fleming, a resident of St. Augustine, received 20,000 acres of
land along the Indian River. Reproduced on this page is the original survey of
Township 31 South, Range 38 East, drawn in 1844, which shows the southern tip
of the grant jutting into Indian River County. A dotted line running south from
the grant represents a military trail blazed by troops under the command of
General Joseph Hernandez during the Second Seminole War (1835-1842).
Superimposed on the township plat is a 1925 map of Indian River County that
shows the location of the township within the newly formed county.

and drove the Seminoles southward in the peninsula. Subsequent treaties between the United States and the Seminole Nation served only to delay an almost inevitable second conflict. The 1823 Treaty of Moultrie Creek ceded tribal lands in north Florida to the United States but gave the Seminoles control over much of the southern peninsula. The Treaty of Payne's Landing, concluded in 1832, required the Seminoles to move west of the Mississippi within three years. Militant tribal leaders—among them Osceola, Coacoochee, Micanopy, Alligator, and Arpieka—opposed the treaty. They did not want to surrender their lands or the Negroes who lived among them.

Hostilities erupted in December 1835 when the Seminoles began destroying the sugar plantations south of St. Augustine. Almost to a person, the inhabitants of lands along the Florida east coast fled to St. Augustine. The abandoned sugar industry never recovered. Ordered by federal authorities to suppress the rebellion and force compliance with the 1832 treaty, the United States Army began to construct throughout the theater of peninsular war a series of fortifications and supply stations, linked by military roads hacked out of the wilderness. One of them, Fort Pierce, arose just south of the Indian River Inlet in 1837. Named for its commander, Lt. Colonel Benjamin Kendrick Pierce, brother of the future president, Franklin Pierce, the fort remained in service for five years. During that time, William T. Sherman and Joseph E. Johnston, who would later face each other in battle during the Civil War, spent short tours of duty at the remote fort. The most noteworthy event that involved troops from Fort Pierce during the war was the capture of a Seminole leader, Chief Wildcat.

A brutal, protracted conflict that dragged on for seven years, the war engaged fewer than two thousand Seminole warriors against federal military forces that numbered more than 9,000 men. It exacted a dreadful cost in civilian and military casualties on both sides, high financial expense, and destruction of considerable property. At its end, nearly 4,000 Indians were removed to the territories west of the Mississippi River. A few hundred resisted deportation by hiding out of reach in the Everglades, where they lived to wage yet another fight, a brief and almost uneventful conflict that began and quickly ended in 1858.

The Second Seminole War prompted the Congress in 1842 to adopt the Armed Occupation Act, which provided a legal basis for settling and occupying the former lands of the Indians in the lower part of the peninsula. The law enabled a single man over eighteen years of age, or any head of a household, to claim 160 acres of land south of an imaginary line that ran east-west between Gainesville and Palatka. The occupant was required to maintain a presence on the land for five years, improve at least five acres of the tract, and erect a house. Immigrants had to be capable of bearing arms and could not settle within two miles of a military post. Claims under the new law sprinkled the Indian River region from Barker's Bluff near Sebastian Inlet southward to Jupiter Inlet. Most of the claims were clustered on the west side of the Indian River near Fort Pierce.

By 1844, approximately 1,200 settlers were living in the Indian River region, largely the result of the Armed Occupation Act. One of the first settlements was called Susanna, whose only remnant today is a coquina stone chimney. The domiciles of the first settlers were generally primitive log shelters with palmetto

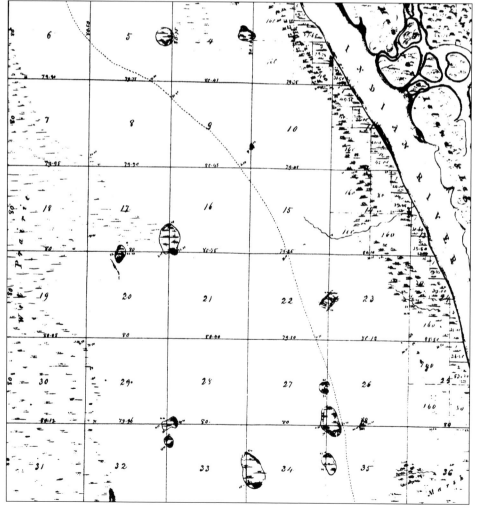

The division of Florida into townships, ranges and sections began early in the Territorial Period. By the mid-1830s, the surveyors had reached the east coast. The savage Second Seminole War (1835-1842) interrupted their activities, which the surveyors resumed quickly at the war's end. They braved swamps, snakes, and swarming mosquitoes as they stretched their measurement chains across the virgin land. The accompanying map is the original survey of Township 32 South, Range 39 East, located immediately above the township that today holds Vero Beach. The township now contains Gifford and Winter Beach. The dotted line running through the township shows the continuation of the military road known as the General Hernandez Trail.

frond thatched roofs. Colonel Samuel H. Peck of Augusta, Georgia, was one of the few settlers to construct a wood frame house. Peck later sold his property to Captain Miles O. Burnham, who began growing pineapples on a farm at Ankona Bluff. Other noteworthy settlers included Ossian B. Hart, a future governor of Florida and Dr. Holbrook, a Charleston physician. The remaining residents in the rudimentary community included carpenters, sailors, and slaves. In 1844, a year before Florida joined the Union, the Territorial Legislature chiseled Santa Lucia County out of Mosquito County. The new county reached from Cape Canaveral southward to Lake Worth. The Kissimmee River formed its western boundary. Passage into the new county remained difficult. U.S. Army Lieutenant Jacob Blake reported to General William J. Worth in 1843 that "the (sand) bar at the mouth of the Indian River does not admit . . . the passage of vessels drawing more than eight feet." The Intracoastal Waterway provided the only practical entrance to the Indian River country. Even there, the haulover for vessels at Mosquito Inlet engendered delay and costly, backbreaking work. Portions of the Indian River were too hazardous for all but narrow, shallow draft schooners. Navigation around Cape Canaveral was deemed dangerous and, in some cases, more expensive than traveling by inland waterways or by land.

Fewer than ten people per square mile inhabited the Indian River region on the eve of the Civil War. Slaves comprised about one-third of the population. Most of the widely scattered farmers practiced subsistence agriculture, eighty percent of them on farms less than fifty acres in size. Only one percent of the farms embraced 500 acres or more, a size large enough to qualify as a plantation. Rice and sugarcane constituted the major commercial crops. In 1855, Santa Lucia County was renamed Brevard County. Reconstitution of counties would continue for another sixty-five years before Indian River County finally emerged in 1925.

Chapter Two
Civil War, Reconstruction, and Early Settlement, 1861-1892

A BLOCKADE OF SOUTHERN WATERS TO INTERRUPT CONFEDERATE TRADE and communications formed a major part of the Union's naval strategy during the Civil War. To the extent that the war visited Indian River County, it came in the form of engagements between Union forces and blockade runners. U.S. Secretary of the Navy Gideon Welles in June 1862 ordered Union steamships of the East Gulf Blockading Squadron to patrol Florida's Atlantic coastline. Although early reconnaissance indicated that the shallow bars and narrow channels at the local inlets would impede entry ocean-bound traffic, Confederate blockade runners did manage periodically to navigate the channels.

The Union vessels patrolling the Indian River environs included the *U.S.S. Beauregard, U.S.S. Gem of the Sea, U.S.S. Pursuit,* and *U.S.S. Sagamore.* Because of its relatively large size, the *Beauregard,* was unable to navigate either of the two local inlets leading into the Indian River and thus had to remain at sea. Instead, the *Gem of the Sea* and *Sagamore* regularly patrolled those waters in place of the *Beauregard.* A bark with four masts, the *Gem of the Sea* measured one hundred sixteen feet long and weighed three hundred seventy-one tons. Armament consisted of four three-pound cannons and one twenty pound Parrot rifle. The heavier *Sagamore,* equipped with two steam boilers, screw propellers, and two masts, could only occasionally navigate through the inlets. The boat weighed nearly twice as much as the *Gem of the Sea* and sported a twenty pound Parrot rifle, twelve inch Dahlgren smooth bore cannon, two twenty-four pound howitzers, and a twelve pound cannon.

In late February 1863, after making its way through the inlet at high tide and then finding cover in a cove near the Sebastian River, the crew of the gunboat *Sagamore* seized the English blockade runner *Charm* "at a place called the Narrows," a several miles-long stretch of the Indian River near the present-day location of Wabasso. Five of the arrested crewmen protested the seizure, claiming they were "endeavoring to escape the late rebel conscript act." Their pleas fell on

This 1863 line drawing from **Harper's Weekly** depicts a typical Union gun boat that plied the waters of Florida's Atlantic coast during the Civil War.

deaf ears. The *Gem of the Sea* carried blockade runner Captain Titus (for whom Titusville was later named), his crew, passengers, and thirty-five bales of cotton to Key West. Following the raid, Lieutenant Baxter of the *Sagamore* reported "I think the blockade running at this station is about broken up for the present; there has not a vessel run in at either of the inlets without being captured since we came on this station, and but two have got out; they were two small sloops having on board, each of them, 13 bales of cotton and a few passengers."

In March 1863, Rear Admiral Theodorus Bailey reported to Secretary Welles that Henry A. Crane and seven other residents of the Indian River region had assisted federal sailors aboard the gunboats *Gem of the Sea* and *Sagamore* in the capture of blockade runners. Bailey cited their bravery and "efficient service in clearing out rebels from Indian River and in breaking up their connection with the lawless traders of Nassau . . . . It is scarcely too much to say," emphasized Bailey, "that without the local knowledge and personal acquaintance[s] possessed by these men it would have been nearly impossible to effect this very desirable object." Bailey reported a blockade runner at Sand Point (later-day Titusville), but believed it drew too much water to sail before the river reached high tide.

Tidal influences and shifting bars hampered movements of Federal boats and blockade runners. Federal boats periodically sailed the Indian River as far north as the Sebastian River. Little further blockade running activities were reported by the East Gulf Blockading Squadron, outside the immediate vicinity of the Indian River or Jupiter inlets. Still, Federal naval officers sailed Union vessels through the inlets "whenever the bar will permit them to cross. The bar at Jupiter Inlet," reported Lieutenant Baxter in 1863, "is nearly dry at low water."

One final incident occurred in June 1863, at a point near present-day Oslo. The sloop *Kate,* from Nassau, was captured with its crew and cargo by the bark *U.S.S. Pursuit.* Lieutenant Randall of the *Pursuit* sent the *Kate* for adjudication to Key West and reported the names of his crew entitled to a share of the captured cargo. By the close of the war, Federal gunboats had seized various contraband along the Indian River, including candles, coffee, cotton, flour, gin, matches, salt, and tea. Hardly a cannon shot had been fired along the Indian River during the war. By 1864, the *Sagamore* had been reassigned to Florida's Gulf Coast. In one dramatic episode published in *Harper's Weekly,* the crew of the *Sagamore* adeptly outsailed and then destroyed by cannon fire two Rebel schooners near the Homassassa River.

Most Floridians welcomed the war's end and the opportunity to return to a normal life, though the economy had suffered. The transportation network lay in shambles. Most roads in East Florida were little more than dirt paths, some of them remnants of military trails carved through the woods and swamps during the Second Seminole War. Miles of iron rails in north Florida were rusted and their roadbeds, neglected for years, overgrown. Although Florida was perceived as an attractive state for railroad construction, party rivalries in state government pitted interstate rivals against intrastate factions, hampering the organization of companies and killing projected construction projects.

Organized in the 1850s, the Internal Improvement Fund (IIF), which held title to state lands, had become mired in debt. Because state law stipulated that no land could be conveyed until the debt was cleared, the fund's trustees began searching for investors who would help eliminate the deficit. Through the connections of Governor William Bloxham, they began negotiations with multi-millionaire Hamilton Disston, a Philadelphia steel magnate who had visited Florida in 1877. Disston agreed to purchase four million acres in central and south Florida for $1 million. Known historically as the Disston Purchase, the transaction included vast tracts between Lake Tohopekaliga in central Florida and Fort Myers in southwest Florida.

The sale permitted the state government to subsidize rail construction through the award of real estate to railroad companies. Eventually, the trustees distributed some 9 million acres in rail subsidies. By 1901, following one of largest land grabs in Florida history, relatively little public

Pulling into Nassau, this Confederate blockade runner was typical of the ships that carried cargoes from the Indian River region during the war. Most ships this size could sail the river only after navigating the unpredictable inlets at high tide.

domain remained to encourage private development. On the other hand, the state's rail mileage expanded from 518 to 2,500 miles between 1880 and 1890. Tracks soon provided efficient transportation into the peninsula and along the coasts, reaching places hitherto considered a virtually impenetrable wilderness. Despite the economic turbulence of the nineteenth century's last decade, Florida's rail system continued to grow, reaching 3,200 miles in 1900.

The railroad permitted the fast export of oranges and it brought into the state hordes of speculators and settlers filled with visions of citrus fortune. The original "orange belts" of Florida extended along the St. Johns River and the upper Indian River, but a new "golden crescent" of groves began to lengthen from the Indian River to Tampa Bay. Present-day Indian River County, which lay outside that region, experienced only moderate growth and agricultural development at the time. Not until Henry Flagler brought his railroad south from Jacksonville would the state's lower east coast emerge from its relative isolation.

In the mid-1870s, the state's east coast came to the attention of the U.S. Life-Saving Service, a predecessor of the U.S. Coast Guard. In June 1874, the Congress authorized a system of houses of refuge along Florida's east coast, which, the service reported, "differs in its conditions, and in the character of the life-saving aid . . . from any other coast of the United States. Its conformation is such that vessels driven ashore come so near the beach as to enable their crews to gain the land by their own efforts with comparatively little difficulty, and without any considerable hazard of drowning . . . . But those who gain the shore are then in danger of perishing by hunger and thirst, the coast being entirely desolate and with hardly an inhabitant." New legislation called for the provision of shelters and food for shipwrecked mariners. By April 1876, five houses of refuge had been constructed. The first of them, later known as Bethel Creek House of Refuge, was located on the beach thirteen miles north of Indian River Inlet, in the vicinity of what in the late twentieth century became Jaycee Park in Vero Beach.

The houses of refuge, about 25 miles apart, were each staffed by a keeper. They provided accommodations for twenty-five people and provisions to feed shipwreck victims for ten days. Additional houses were soon constructed at Gilbert's Bar (near present-day Stuart), Orange Grove (Delray Beach), Fort Lauderdale, and Biscayne Bay. Wooden mile markers between the buildings helped guide survivors to the nearest refuge. U.S. Treasury records and daily journals of keepers confirm a dreary, isolated life along the desolate beach. Few remained long. The Bethel Creek outpost registered four keepers in its first ten years. They responded to wrecks, stranded ships, and distress calls from private launches along the river and ocean. Grave markers near the building testified that some shipwrecked victims did not survive.

The Bethel Creek outpost was converted to a coast guard station about 1915, when the Life-Saving Service was consolidated into the U.S. Coast Guard. The Bethel Creek House of Refuge burned in 1917. The Coast Guard remained at work on the property, however, retreating to another dwelling located west of what had been the House of Refuge. In some years, especially those associated with Prohibition, a crew of five with a cutter were stationed there, primarily to intercept smugglers importing alcohol and narcotics from the Bahamas.

Florida drew a rising number of visitors after 1865. National publishers capitalized on the state's popularity as a vacation destination with a flurry of guidebooks. Although they say little about the remote and sparsely settled Indian River region, the books do offer a glimpse of conditions at the time. Philadelphia physician and medical journal editor Daniel Brinton published one of the first in 1869, *A Guide-Book of Florida and the South for Tourists, Invalids and Emigrants.* He recommended that "persons wishing to visit Indian river for camp hunting, should hire an open boat, guide, and tent at Jacksonville, and bring them to Enterprise on the steamer. From that point they can row to Lake Harney in two days, where the boat and tent can be carried across to Sand Point, on Indian river, on an ox team."

> ### Francis Chandler & Bethel Creek House of Refuge
>
> Francis Chandler of Boston, a gifted architect who later taught at M.I.T., prepared a standardized plan for the houses of refuge. They were built along utilitarian lines, fifteen feet wide and thirty-seven feet long with a gable roof, two shed dormers, double-hung sash windows, a veranda that wrapped around three elevations, clapboard siding, and brick piers. Carpenters built ten dwellings based on Chandler's specifications along Florida's east coast between 1876 and 1885. Contractor Albert Blaisdell of Boston assembled the first five at an approximate cost of $3000 each. At Bethel Creek, Blaisdell and his carpenters reportedly landed building materials on the beach only after a great deal of difficulty negotiating the tide and currents; the house was completed in February 1876.

Poet laureate Sidney Lanier, daunted by the difficult route to the Indian River, chose to sail other, more accessible inland rivers. In his *Florida: Its Scenery, Climate, and History* (1875) Lanier observed that "The common method of reaching the Indian River country is by stage from Enterprise, on the St. Johns; or by small steamer from Enterprise to Salt Lake; thence by wheels to Sand Point."

*James Henshall navigated the **Blue Wing** along the Indian River in 1878. His sloop was typical of those used by Florida tourists during the 1870s and 1880s. This sketch portrays Henshall's vessel at Jupiter lighthouse.*

Lanier pointed out that the steamer *Pioneer* had been plying the length of the Indian River since the early 1870s, and that a second steamer, the *Mayflower*, was scheduled for service in 1876. Lanier encouraged travel to the Indian River, where the "waters are full of fish in great variety; the woods abound in deer and other game; and the whole land amounts to perpetual invitation to the overworked, the invalid, the air-poisoned, the nervously prostrate people, to come down with yacht and tent, with rod and gun, and rebuild brain, muscle, and nerve."

Chicago newspaper journalist George Barbour published a series of guide books to the state, based largely on observations he made while on tour in 1879 with Gen. Ulysses S. Grant. Since Barbour traveled the river only as far south as Rockledge, his knowledge of the Indian River country was limited. He noted that the St. Sebastian River drained the inland region known as the Halpatiokee Flats, a Native American name for the area near the future site of Fellsmere.

Another physician, James Henshall of Cincinnati, Ohio, launched the eighteen-foot yacht *Blue Wing* from Titusville in December 1878. Accompanied by five friends and equipped with tents, rifles, blankets, and medical equipment, Henshall arrived in the Indian River region a year later. He provided the best of all descriptions about the late nineteenth century Indian River region. In his account, *Camping and Cruising in Florida,* Henshall wrote:

"At the mouth of the St. Sebastian we passed the fine hamack [sic] of Mr. Gibson, and a few miles below we arrived at Barker's Bluff, quite an eminence, on which is the cabin of Arthur Park. Opposite here is Pelican Island, a few acres in extent, and first of a series of islands forming the Narrows. The mangroves and water-oaks of this island have been all killed by the excrement of the pelicans which breed there. This guano, which lies several inches deep on the ground, is utilized by the settlers as an efficient fertilizer. As we passed, we saw a party of northern tourists at the island, shooting down the harmless birds by scores through mere wantonness. As volley after volley came booming over the water, we felt quite disgusted at the useless slaughter, and bore away as soon as possible. . . ."

Henshall visited Key West in 1882, and also sailed the **Rambler** *up the South Prong of the St. Sebastian River.*

On a second trip in January 1882, Henshall sailed the Indian River in the five-ton schooner *Rambler*. On the banks of the St. Sebastian River, his party stumbled across a Seminole camp, complete with deer-skin scaffolds. Henshall again visited Pelican Island and farther downriver met Captain Estes at the Narrows. Henshall fondly recounted that Estes, in 1876, had displayed two manatees from local waters to the Centennial Exposition in Philadelphia.

Few writers adequately described the hardships endured by Florida's early settlers. The first Sebastian settler, August Park, a native of Danzig, Germany, arrived in the 1860s with a contract from the Florida Canning Company of New York to pack fish for northern markets. He eventually settled near the St. Sebastian River and built a house on Barker's Bluff, several miles south on the Indian River, where he also operated a turtle fishery and a trading post. Inland, he started the community's first cemetery. Park died in 1895, and his heirs platted Park's subdivision in 1907.

The Kroegel family made Sebastian its home in 1881. Charles Freidrich Gottlob Kroegel left Germany in 1871 and worked in New York and Chicago for a time before moving to Fernandina and then the Indian River region. He purchased his first piece of land on Barker's Bluff south of Sebastian from August

Shell Roads

In January 1895 the *Indian River Advocate,* published in Titusville and one of the first newspapers published within the Indian River region, capitalized on a fierce debate over road construction. Tongue-in-cheek, the newspaper related "the mound, in its present state, shows a clear cut section, from crown to base lengthwise, and streets of shell alternate with those of ashes and bones." The following week, the columnist predictably recanted his prose, exclaiming that ". . . in last week's issue, the *Advocate* printed streets instead of strata. This was, no doubt, caused by the prevailing shell-road agitation." The editor explained his play-on-words played on the tensions between residents of the mainland, who enjoyed both a railroad and good shell roads, while peninsula dwellers could not "even boast of a trail connecting the different settlements . . . from Canaveral south." Indeed, only the faintest of outlines of the county's present-day road system had appeared in the late nineteenth century. Roads on the mainland largely followed military trails established decades earlier; peninsular roadways largely followed section and range lines, meandering between homesteads and citrus groves.

Park. The bluff, an ancient aboriginal shell mound, was reportedly 1,000 feet long, 400 feet wide, and 100 feet high. Kroegel built his house on the bluff and planted truck crops and orange trees around it. Kroegel sold a portion of the bluff in 1908 to St. Lucie County, which mined its contents for road-building material.

Residents of the region had harvested ancestral shell mounds for roadbeds since the 1890s. "Two Dollar Bluff," thought to be Barker's Bluff, was among the first to go. One son of the Kroegel family, Paul Kroegel, became renowned for his fierce protection of native pelicans. A skilled carpenter, he built several houses for Kroegel family members and fabricated the sloop *Audubon* for Guy Bradley, an Audubon Society warden. He served on the St. Lucie Board of County Commissioners between 1905 and 1918. To help protect Florida's pelicans, he enlisted the assistance of Frank Chapman and other renowned ornithologists. His efforts were rewarded in 1903, when President Theodore Roosevelt designated Pelican Island as a federal reservation. Kroegel was appointed warden of the island.

The Park and Kroegel families arrived at Sebastian in the 1880s. The village centered around a post office established by Thomas New, a retired Methodist preacher. He named the community Newhaven and in April 1882 won appointment as postmaster. He was replaced in November 1884 by an English immigrant, Sylvanus Kitching, who renamed the community Sebastian. In 1881, New cut a shallow inlet through the barrier island. New's Cut, as the inlet became known, served only to facilitate floating large driftwood and salvage from distressed boats across the peninsula to the mainland and accommodated only the smallest of vessels. Interest in the inlet waned after January 1886, when New died.

The Kitching family of Sebastian was part of Florida's nineteenth-century English colony movement. Sylvanus Kitching of Warrington, England, arrived on Florida's east coast in 1883. Earlier, in 1867, brothers Broster, Pennington, and Walter Kitching had immigrated to the United States, eventually settling at Stuart. Sylvanus Kitching selected Sebastian for his new home, setting up a general store and building an 1,100-foot dock on the river for steamboats. After his election as postmaster of Newhaven, he changed the name of the community to Sebastian. An early landmark in Sebastian, Kitching's two-story building contained a general store, living quarters, and accommodations for visitors. His son, Stanley, moved in 1902 to Stuart, where he became a leading merchant and mayor of the city. About 1911 the Kitching settlement was established some four miles southwest of Sebastian. Little more than a saw mill camp, the settlement was briefly a whistle stop on the Fellsmere Railroad and the area was also referred to as Eureka.

Scattered settlement also occurred farther north of Sebastian along the St. Sebastian River, where surveyor S.B. Carter divided the Fleming grant into relatively small parcels for farming and development. The Roseland and Wauregan villages, part of the Fleming grant, stood on a peninsula formed by the south bank of the St. Sebastian River and the west bank of the Indian River. In 1889 the Town of Wauregan was carved out of the grant. The ambitious town plan consisted of ninety blocks, roughly L-shaped, with Sylvanus Kitching's store and dock immediately south of the development. Between the Wauregan town plan and the Indian River stood the homesteads of David P. Gibson, W.J. Knight, and August Park. Although a few settlers, such as W.W. Bissell, T.S. Drake, A.P. Hudson, H.H. Todd, and H.J. Zelm, purchased land in Wauregan, the most significant landholder was the East Coast Turpentine Company. The turpentine company owned most of the land in the Fleming grant, where it harvested the pine forests for naval stores and timber.

Roseland emerged as a place name about 1892, when William Eason was appointed postmaster of the newly-opened post office. Settlement had begun in the 1870s with Dempsey Cain, generally regarded as the community's founder. David P. Gibson, a native of Georgia, established a homestead there in the 1880s. H.D. Ruffner of West Virginia, who arrived in 1896, built a two-story house overlooking the Indian River, like most early settlers. Roseland gradually

Turpentine & Naval Stores

In Florida, the harvesting of pine tree sap, or resin, called "naval stores" for its use as a caulk to seal seams of wooden ships, dates to the First Spanish Period (1565-1763). Spanish and English settlers chipped trees to obtain sap for various uses, but little organized harvesting occurred in the state until after the Civil War. Still, Florida ranked fourth in the nation in its production by 1850, and in the 1890s some settlers reaped great wealth from the natural resource. By 1900, Florida's naval stores industry accounted for 32 percent of the nation's production, and into the 1920s Florida ranked first in output. By 1938, the state produced nearly 20 percent of the product worldwide, but by then Florida's forest wealth had been depleted to one-quarter its volume a century earlier. Most turpentine camps consisted of a fire still, spirit shed and glue pot, rosin yard, blacksmith and cooperage shed, cup-cleaning vat, barn and wagon shed, and living quarters for the manager and workers. During a season, an average camp harvested 50,000 trees, typically utilizing trees with a diameter greater than nine inches. The Florida Naval Stores and Commission Company of Jacksonville, perhaps the largest and earliest naval stores enterprise in the state, was organized in 1899. By 1902, the company owned 250,000 acres of timber and processed naval stores harvested from another 1 million acres controlled by other Florida operators. Indian River County pine trees contributed to Florida's exhaustive output of naval stores between the 1890s and the 1930s.

expanded, taking over some of Wauregan. In 1903, surveyor J.O. Fries created a plan of Roseland, nine blocks along the south bank of the St. Sebastian River. Apparently, the plan failed to attract development. A second town site appeared in 1911, when the Florida Development Company of Clarinda, Iowa, hired John Swann to revise the plan. Swann laid out forty-two blocks along the south bank of the St. Sebastian River, west of the railroad tracks. Streets radiated in a grid pattern with Roseland Street paralleling the tracks. Four blocks were reserved for cottages, a church, a park, and a school. Some houses soon appeared and the Roseland Methodist Church arose in 1916.

In 1886, David Gibson cut an inlet through the peninsula across from Roseland and Sebastian, entering the Atlantic Ocean two-and-one-half-miles north of New's Cut. Ten years later he engineered another improvement to the inlet, but the cut remained little more than a shallow ditch. The Sebastian Inlet Association organized a subsequent dredging of Gibson's Cut in 1899, removing nearly 7,000 cubic feet of material. The ocean soon reclaimed the inlet, however, prohibiting entry even to migrating schools of fish. The U.S. Army Corps of Engineers concluded in 1905 that because of a lack of nearby serviceable inlets "the supply of fish is becoming exhausted, and that the portion above the Narrows especially suffers owing to the large number taken . . ." Some fishermen dragged small boats across the peninsula to get to the ocean. One Sebastian resident observed that because no inlet provided a fresh supply of water, the river would sometimes become stagnant "causing the death of a great quantity of fish which putrefy on the shores and results in a stench both unpleasant and unhealthy."

By 1905 four small inlets had been carved through the peninsula near Sebastian; the Corps deemed only Gibson's Cut worthy of improvement. But, in May 1906, after a comprehensive survey and examination, that plan too was abandoned. Frank Forster of Orchid expressed concern that a substantial inlet might cause flooding of lowlands. Cost was a factor. It would have required some $125,000 to complete the dredging. Moreover, the need for an inlet to accommodate steamboats had largely evaporated. The railroad by then offered a speedier and less expensive means to transport fish and oranges to northern markets.

The region attracted out-of-state investors. Seven residents of New York City incorporated the Indian River Land & Improvement Company in 1888. The Albany, Georgia-based Sheffield Land & Investment Company acquired property in the Fleming grant in 1890. Several years later, in 1893, the Sebastian River Land & Improvement Company of New York was incorporated by New Rochelle, New York, residents Thomas Drake, Alexander Hudson, and Henri Van Zelm. The firms invested heavily in Sebastian area real estate and engaged in naval stores harvesting. James A. Hudson of Jefferson County, Arkansas, tried his hand at property development, opening subdivisions north of Sebastian in 1891 and 1897. Hudson's First Addition spread along the Indian River, providing large acreage riverfront lots. A second plat extended five blocks west of the railroad tracks; he named the streets Arkansas, Division, Edwards, Hudson, and Ring. For several years, Hudson enjoyed relatively brisk land sales, especially along the waterfront.

Indian River Narrows justifiably claims the second oldest permanent area of settlement in Indian River County. Writing in 1879, physician James

J. F. LeBaron

Nineteenth-century surveys of the Indian River by the U.S. Army Corps of Engineers revealed a frontier sparsely settled. Based in Jacksonville, Florida, assistant engineer J.F. LeBaron reported that Haulover Canal, built in 1853, was the first significant improvement along the Indian River. In 1869 he counted about a dozen settlers in a twenty mile radius of Haulover Canal and Mosquito Lagoon. A decade later, studying the Indian River for the Museum of Comparative Zoology at Harvard University, LeBaron still found few settlers and little development. In 1881 he estimated that 1600 people occupied homesteads in the region between Haulover Canal and the south end of Lake Worth. Along the Indian River he counted thirteen stores and eight post offices, and reported that "this region is comparatively unknown and generally supposed to be given over to alligators and mosquitoes."

Henshall began his description of the locale by noting that "Pelican Island, a few acres in extent, [is the] first of a series of islands forming the Narrows . . . which is some ten miles in length, and from an eighth to a half mile in width; the channel is about a hundred yards from the western shore or mainland." Henshall continued:

> "There are numerous oyster-beds and reefs lying but a few inches below the surface of the water . . . . The scenery in the Narrows is quite pleasing. On the right, the mainland is a level bank, clothed with mangroves and water-oaks, with occasional patches of rushes and saw-grass, while in the background can be seen alternations of pine woods and hamaks, which once in a while run down to the river bank . . . . At the lower end of the Narrows is a staked channel leading off through the islands to the left, to the United States Life-Saving Station, No. 1, on the sea-beach, in charge of Mr. John Houston."

Henshall reported few houses in the vicinity, but spotted turtle camps conducting a thriving business between the foot of the Narrows and Fort Pierce. Green turtles caught in gill nets varied in weight from twenty to one hundred pounds. Penned in circular enclosures, the reptiles were later shipped through Titusville and Jacksonville to northern markets. Lewis Dawson opened the Narrows post office in 1884 on Gem Island, north of the Bethel Creek House of Refuge. Dawson, who served aboard the Union gunboat *Gem of the Sea* during the Civil War, returned later to settle upon the Narrows and gave the name Gem Isle to the place where he lived. It was later renamed Barker Island. The *East Coast Advocate* reported that Dawson's home and extensive garden made "Gem Isle blossom like a rose." Chatterbox columns in the *Advocate* initially clustered the activities of residents on the peninsula under the heading "Narrows"; gradually, as settlements at Enos, Narrows, and Orchid were established, they won their own individual columns. In the 1890s Jonathan Bradford, Florida's state engineer, measured the length of the Narrows as nine-and-one-half-miles and placed its north end four miles south of Sebastian and the Narrows post office eight miles south of the river trading center.

The Narrows offered attractive sites for early settlers. John LaRoche, who arrived in 1880, subdivided and named John LaRoche's Island, or Johns Island.

Calvin J. and William N. Reams invested heavily in island real estate in 1890. A short-lived Reams post office opened in 1892, but it was closed four years later and moved north to the Narrows office. Louis Harris served as the Johns Island postmaster, then as agent for the Indian River Steamboat Company. When the steamboat business declined, Harris left the island to work at a mainland express agency. A school was organized on Johns Island in 1893. Calvin Reams leased a site on the island to the primitive Baptists in 1904. A cemetery containing the graves of early settlers remains in use on Johns Island in the twenty-first century. It provides a visible reminder of the nineteenth century settlement.

After purchasing land on the Narrows in 1886, James and Amelia Enos of Illinois set about clearing land for orange and banana trees. Although Enos sold some of his property to the development company of Wise, Harvey & Sears, he reserved the choicest parcels for his Town of Enos, laid out in 1888. One of the most creative early subdivisions along the Indian River, the Enos plan provided 150 lots that extended from river to ocean. Along with several parks, a quirky arrangement of circular lots appeared in block twelve near the river. The scenic location attracted, among others, Ida Hunt of Washington, D.C. and James Dodge of Vineland, New Jersey, who purchased lots in 1889. Other investors and prospective home owners soon followed. Enthusiasm for further development and land purchases was

---

Houses of Refuge

The houses of refuge built along the southeast Florida coast drew the attention of two national magazines, *Lippincott* and *Harper's New Monthly Magazine*, which described them in a series of articles that appeared during the 1870s and 1880s. Assigned to duty in October 1876, John Houston became the first keeper at Bethel Creek. A relative of renowned Texan Sam Houston, John was born in Mayport, Florida, lived briefly in Enterprise, Florida, and ran the Federal blockade between Jupiter and Nassau during the Civil War. After settling in Eau Gallie with other family members, he applied for the keeper position at Bethel Creek, which he held for five years. Most of Houston's reports were repetitious observations of the weather, surf, and conditions at the house. In August 1880, he recorded that the "boathouse at this station was blown down on Sunday morning 29th of August at 4 o'clock by the heaviest gale that I ever saw." Later, in October 1887, Keeper William Stoeckel reported the grounding of the Spanish steamer *Panama,* which managed to resume its passage after the crew jettisoned most of its cargo. A British ship, *Breconshire,* sank south of Bethel House of Refuge in 1894. The entire crew survived. The boiler of the ship can be seen at low tide from Humiston Park. Ludvig Hovelsrud assumed duties at the Bethel Creek post in November 1900, but died three years later after drinking contaminated rainwater collected in a rotten wooden tank.

dampened by a hurricane in 1893. The arrival of the railroad subsequently lured residents back to the mainland, mortally wounding James Enos's town plan. After 1898, when the settlement was renamed Stanwood by a new postmaster, James Dodge, the name Enos faded from local memory.

Two miles north of Enos lies the village of Orchid, whose humble roots endured into the twentieth century. Orchid became a place name about 1887, when Susan Mohr opened a post office at the site. Frank Forster assumed management of the office sixteen months later. The early landholders included T.R. Brownell, A.B. Goodnow, N.B. Hamilton, Langley and Susan Kitching, W.H. Martin, and L. Swab. G.W. King's bee-keeping business produced eight tons of honey in 1894. Decades later, the Deerfield Groves Company adopted the name Orchid for one of its citrus crate labels.

Vermont native Henry Gifford became in 1891 the first postmaster of the nascent settlement of Vero. The origin of the name for the post office remains uncertain. Sarah Gifford supposedly selected the Latin word "vero," or truth. Three decades later, in an attempt to attract prospective settlers and developers, the Vero Board of Trade issued a promotional brochure with a full-color inscription reading "Vero: The Translation of the Word from the Latin is To Speak the Truth." By any measure, present-day Indian River County remained a frontier on the eve of the railroad's arrival. In 1880 Brevard County contained about 1,500 people along 200 miles of Florida coastline. Settlements near tributaries of the Indian River and scattered homesteads sprinkled an otherwise unbroken wilderness. Even the railroad failed to attract large numbers of settlers to present-day Indian River County. The 1900 census counted 196 residents around Sebastian and 100 in the area south of Woodley. As late as 1901, settler W.R. Duncan wrote that Vero contained little more than the Gifford home and a post office. The truly spectacular growth of the region remained two decades away.

Chapter Three
Railroads and Reform, 1893-1910

HENRY FLAGLER'S FLORIDA EAST COAST RAILWAY (FEC) transformed Florida's economy and geography. A former partner of John D. Rockefeller in the Standard Oil Company, Flagler retired to St. Augustine in 1886, where he plunged into the railroad and hotel business. He originally intended to make a winter resort of the Ancient City, converting the small town into the "Newport of the South," a vacation destination for wealthy northerners who would travel there on his railroad. Within a decade, however, he set his sights on the warmer, southeast coast of Florida and began extending his railway along the peninsula. As the line crept southward, one settlement after another arose in its wake. The FEC crawled through Daytona Beach in 1892 and Sebastian the following year. Undaunted by a storm which swept away the Sebastian bridge in October 1893, the rail line eventually reached Lake Worth in 1894 and Miami in 1896. The first train pulled into Sebastian in December 1893. The railroad's completion linked the populous cities of the northeastern coast to the southern tip of Florida and initiated an epoch of growth that has not yet ceased to wane.

Flagler gave little thought to the Indian River region as he built his railroad. He looked almost exclusively at Palm Beach and Miami, where large hotels that he had constructed awaited the winter visitors. But his company also managed a land development business and sought to attract farmers and settlers as buyers of the acreage that the state had allotted the FEC to subsidize construction costs. Lured by glowing descriptions of inexpensive homesteads and fertile lands, waves of settlers arrived. They raised winter vegetables, such as tomatoes, beans, and peppers, as well as citrus fruits, to satisfy northern markets that Flagler's railroad for the first time brought within reach of south Florida's agricultural fields. The cities that today line the FEC tracks in Indian River County almost universally began as agricultural communities at the turn of the century.

credit

An extraordinary entrepreneur and visionary businessman, Henry Flagler (1836-1913) transformed the landscape, society, and economy of Florida. His legacy remains in cities and towns he created along the entire length of the east coast of Florida.

The railroad's arrival spelled an end to the steamboat. The Indian River Steamboat Company, organized in Titusville during the Reconstruction era, serviced thirty-five Indian River settlements by 1893, including Roseland, Sebastian, Orchid, Enos, and Narrows. The steamers *St. Lucie* and *St. Sebastian* made two round-trips weekly between Titusville and Jupiter, a one-way journey of nearly twenty-four hours. Smaller steamers included the *Georgiana, Progress, St. Augustine,* and *White,* which plied the river daily in nine-hour trips between Titusville and Melbourne. Unable to compete with the far speedier railroad, most Indian River steamship companies vanished in bankruptcy.

The railroad also produced changes in settlement patterns. One settler contributing to the Enos chatterbox column in the *East Coast Advocate* wrote in 1897 that "During the steamboat days, the east side was more prominent and the rich hammock lands attracted the attention of strangers, and many who visited this portion of the river became settlers . . . . the construction of the railroad on the west side of the river has thrown a temporary shadow over the peninsula and stopped, for a time, contemplated improvements . . ." As it turned out, many of the "contemplated improvements" never emerged, at least not until the 1920s, when a new crowd of investors sought to remake parts of the peninsula into a fashionable seasonal resort for wealthy northerners.

A devastating frost in the winter of 1894-1895 ravaged many groves. In the early morning hours of December 29, 1894 temperatures dipped throughout Florida, reaching 19 degrees in Rockledge. The cold ruined many vegetable fields, stripped the leaves from trees, and caused oranges to drop from their branches. A warm interval followed, promoting the flow of sap through the trees. Then, on the morning of February 8, 1895, temperatures again dropped sharply and held well below freezing for hours. Even in Key West residents reported a light frost. Northeast Florida's citrus industry, killed to the core, never recovered. But at Orchid, where the relatively warm waters of the Indian River and the Atlantic Ocean embrace the peninsula and provide some relief from the cold, the temperature dipped only to a mere twenty-eight degrees, hardly damaging. Indian River County, in fact, escaped relatively intact.

Of Florida's 3 million mature orange trees standing in 1893, only some 90,000 survived the great freeze. The production of oranges fell from 2.5 million boxes of fruit to less than 150,000 in the years before and after the catastrophe. Many growers in northeast Florida simply abandoned their farms. But most Indian River planters chose to remain and replanted their groves. The region from Sebastian to Oslo soon gained prominence for its citrus. Exchanges associated with statewide organizations such as the Florida Citrus Exchange and American Fruit Growers and local businesses organized by the Gifford, Graves, Helseth, Porcher, Michael, and Sexton interests entered an era of expansion that converted the Indian River region into one of the world's centers of citrus production.

The region's institutions grew along with its population and economy. Between 1884 and 1905, the Brevard County Board of Public Instruction, organized in 1872, built small, wood frame school houses in Orchid, Johns Island, Quay, Roseland, and Sebastian. Over the next decade, more schools appeared in Eureka, Oslo, and Wabasso, along with a second school in Sebastian. County superintendent R.E. Mims said in 1902 that "Our territory is wide and sparsely settled.

Axel Hallstrom

A native of Sweden, Axel Hallstrom left his homeland in 1893, first settling in Berlin and London before immigrating to the United States. Trained to cultivate plants in greenhouses and raised orchards, Hallstrom briefly worked for railroad baron James J. Hill in St. Paul, Minnesota. He left Hill's employment for the Indian River region, where glowing reports from fellow Scandinavians at the Oslo and Viking settlements (the latter now Indrio) encouraged him to try his hand at agriculture in the southern United States. In 1904, he moved his family to Oslo, acquired land, and planted 100,000 pineapple plants. The lure of citrus and fierce competition from Cuban pineapple farmers diverted his interest to plant citrus groves and then invest in banks. In 1914, he purchased stock in the St. Lucie County Bank. Later, he served on the bank's board of directors and then as president. In 1961, Hallstrom given royal honors by His Majesty King Gustav for his service to the Swedish American community. Hallstrom initiated construction of a brick dwelling in Oslo in 1915 and completed it in 1923. The impressive two-story house stands at 1723 SE Old Dixie Highway. His daughter, Ruth Hallstrom, resided there until her death in 1999, and bequeathed the historic residence to the Indian River County Historical Society. The house and accompanying barn and outbuildings contribute to America's legacy of Swedish immigration, most commonly associated with settlements in the midwest.

The people do not favor [consolidation of schools] as yet, but it will come with us in due time as it has already in various sections." Mims inventoried three log buildings and forty-three wood frame school buildings in Brevard County's education system. Most contained only one or two rooms. After 1905, when St. Lucie County was carved out of Brevard County, the new school board continued to consolidate its system, constructing fewer but larger buildings.

Consolidation of the school system was not without problems. One school board member, C.P. Platts, wrote in 1906 that "At one of the schools where this has been adopted it has caused friction practically from the start . . . . the loss of the individual school to . . .a neighboring community, is rather more than some of the patrons can stand." Teachers' wages ranged between $35 and $100 per month. Board member W.J. Nesbitt said in 1908 that consolidation was progressing, though hampered by poor roads and "much ignorance . . . among the parents." Pupils at Indian River Narrows were drawn from within a radius of five miles. From the mainland, students walked each day to the river where they were collected in launches and transported to the Johns Island school.

The turn of the century's Progressive movement created many changes in American society. Perhaps the era's most striking event locally was land reclamation, which promoted agricultural expansion. Huge investments by northern businessmen resulted in extensive drainage operations, intensive publicity campaigns, and town plans for Fellsmere and Vero, all of which encouraged the formation of commercial centers and surrounding residential neighborhoods. By the end of the "Great War" in 1918, citrus had come to dominate the economy and the landscape, with miles of groves branching out in all directions.

Conservation was another reform of the time. Between 1903 and 1909, President Theodore Roosevelt established by executive order fifty-one national bird reservations in the United States. One presidential biographer has suggested that no "President, before or since, or the head of any other government for that matter, has ever taken such as interest in the avian folk of the world." Angered by the slaughtered birds in Florida and elsewhere, often cloaked in the guise of sport hunting or for plumes to supply the millinery trade, Roosevelt acted to formulate protective bird legislation. The first few national bird sanctuaries, since renamed national wildlife refuges, included Pelican Island, Florida. The Florida Legislature also took a stand, adopting a bill protecting "gulls, terns, plume and all other wild birds, also their nests and eggs at all times."

The Kroegel Family

Paul Kroegel

The Kroegel family arrived in Sebastian in 1881. Gottlob Kroegel immigrated from Germany in 1870, first living in New York City, then Chicago, and finally Sebastian, where he built a home at Barker's Bluff. The bluff, really a shell mound with an aboriginal heritage, measured 1,000 feet long and 400 feet wide. Settlers throughout Florida used shell mounds during the late nineteenth century for home sites and often sold the material to road construction companies. At Sebastian, the Kroegels raised vegetables and planted citrus. The family was said to have planted the first orange grove in Indian River County. One son, Paul Kroegel, became renowned for his fierce love and protection of native pelicans. A skilled carpenter, he built several houses for Kroegel family members and fabricated the sloop *Audubon* for Guy Bradley, an Audubon Society warden who was later murdered by poachers. To help protect Florida's pelicans, he enlisted the assistance of renowned scientists, including Frank Chapman and George Nelson. His efforts were rewarded in 1903, when President Theodore Roosevelt designated Pelican Island as a federal reservation. Development and erosion at the close of the 20th century prompted the U.S. Fish & Wildlife Service, in partnership with universities, government agencies, historical societies, non-profit organizations, and corporations, to preserve a precious resource that Paul Kroegel fought to save nearly 100 years ago. In 1995, photographer James Culberson helped immortalize the Kroegel family when he published *Images Through the Doors of Time,* a photographic extravaganza of the Kroegels and the Sebastian area. Those photographs were reproduced from glass slides taken by Paul Kroegel's son, Rodney.

Local controversy over the killing of non-game birds had simmered for years. As early as 1893, The *Indian River Advocate* carried an editorial by DeWitt Webb from the hamlet of Atlantic, located north of Sebastian, decrying the high prices paid by northern designers for plumes, which he said tempted poachers to invade rookeries. Webb claimed that "One can sail for fifty miles sometimes on the Indian River without seeing one (pelican), when in the past hundreds might be seen." W.T. Hornaday of Micco reported that hunters in a steam launch and two sail boats had visited Pelican Island in April 1894 and killed hundreds of birds. He insisted that "authorities of Brevard county, and of the state of Florida make a great mistake in failing to preserve that rookery, and allowing brutal and unscrupulous gunners to slaughter the birds on that island."

The Audubon Society and American Ornithologist's Union focused national attention on the demise of the brown pelican. Professional ornithologists and naturalists from throughout the country periodically visited, wrote about, and photographed Pelican Island. Dr. Morris Gibbs contributed to the debate with his "Nesting Habits of the Brown Pelican in Florida," published in the *Oologist* in March 1894. Gibbs estimated that of 4,000 pelicans inhabiting Pelican Island in 1892, fewer than 1,000 remained in 1894. Other observers recorded declines in the numbers of egrets, ibises, and spoonbills at Cape Sable. An agreement between New York's Millinery Merchant's Protective Association and the Audubon Society of New York to reduce the number of natural feathers used in fashion wear did little to stop the slaughter.

Roosevelt had studied birds since his youth. Approached by a delegation from the Audubon Society about protecting Pelican Island birds, the president turned to his legal advisor and asked, "Is there any law that will prevent me from declaring Pelican Island a Federal Bird Reservation?" A negative response prompted the president to reply, "Very well, then I so declare it." An executive order issued on March 14, 1903 designated Pelican Island as a bird reservation, the first in a system that has since grown to be the most far-reaching and comprehensive wildlife resource management program in the history of mankind. Conducted with little fanfare, the designation initially escaped the attention of the *New York Times* and, locally, even the *Florida Times-Union* in Jacksonville and Titusville's *Indian River Advocate*.

The Department of Agriculture described Pelican Island as "little more than a mud flat, with only a few black mangroves, one or two cabbage palms, and large patches of grass to conceal its expanse . . ." In October 1909, a hurricane flooded the island and forced the birds to move to a new nesting site a short distance away that measured about twenty acres in size. Sustained interest in protecting the birds led in 1909 to a second executive order enlarging the wildlife refuge. Although many hatchlings and eggs perished during severe storms in 1907, 1911, and 1912, the pelicans flourished. The federally protected property was enlarged by four hundred acres in 1969, occupying the islands of Egret, David, Horseshoe, Middle, Nelson, North, Oyster, Paul, Pelican, Preachers, Roosevelt, and Roseate.

County redistricting continued throughout the Progressive Era. Long and narrow, Brevard County, organized in 1855, stretched the entire length of the Indian River, from the St. Lucie River to the northern settlement of Mims, nearly 120 miles in all. As early as 1892, the Brevard County Reform Association had supported relocating the seat of government to a more central site, such as Fort Pierce. Agitation was ceaseless. The editor of the Titusville *Advocate,* Charles Walton, charged in 1905 that the "frenzied politics" and "County Divisionists" of Fort Pierce caused most of the commotion. Indeed, over the objections of Titusville residents, the Florida Legislature acceded to the appeals from the citizens of Fort Pierce and organized St. Lucie County on May 24, 1905. The division carved Brevard County neatly in half. The new county reached from the St. Lucie River to the St. Sebastian River. The arguments portended a similar struggle twenty years later that resulted in the formation of Indian River County.

Fishing emerged as an important local industry during the Progressive era. In 1895, Congress ordered the U.S. Commission of Fish and Fisheries to conduct a comprehensive examination of migratory fishes of the Indian River. Commercial fishing on the river began in 1886 with the arrival in Titusville of the Atlantic Coast, St. Johns, and Indian River Railway. By 1895, nineteen firms between Titusville and Stuart were harvesting seafood from the river and Atlantic waters. Twenty-four species of ocean life supported the industry, primarily mullet, pompano, sheepshead, squetegue, and oysters. Florida law at the time prohibited "the use of seines, gill nets, or other nets, except common cast nets within one

Commercial fishing provided jobs for many people along the Indian River in the early twentieth century. J. H. Hurst managed Vero's Scobie & Co., which operated into the 1920s.

Matthew Quay

U.S. Senator Matthew Quay, Republican boss of Pennsylvania, played a role in President Theodore Roosevelt's designation of Pelican Island as a federal reservation. Quay, who served in the U.S. Senate between 1887 and 1904, maintained a winter residence at St. Lucie Village, some fifteen miles south of Pelican Island. He escaped to his Florida retreat as often as possible to rest and fish for tarpon. Shortly before Quay's death in 1904, the Woodley village was renamed Quay in his honor. Sometime in the 1920s the name Winter Beach replaced Quay. A political ally and friend of Theodore Roosevelt, Quay supported dredging and inlet improvements along the Indian River to the extent that, upon his death, the Jacksonville Florida Times Union eulogized him as "Florida's third Senator."

mile of any pass or inlet." Catches of select species, such as pompano, were shipped to New York, Louisville, or St. Louis; mullet, the most common fish harvested from the river, was shipped to local markets in Florida and Georgia.

Charles Peake of Sebastian began catching turtles in gill nets in 1886. He gathered 2,500 turtles in his first season. A decade later, he complained that overharvesting had resulted in their decline and that steamboats disrupted turtle movements, killing many upon impact. During the great freeze of February 1895, Peake discovered "several hundred turtles . . . floating on the surface in a numbed or frozen condition. On being warmed most of them survived and were soon on their way to the northern markets." Before shipping the turtles, the fisheries confined them in pens and fattened them with vegetables such as sweet potato vines and mangrove leaves. The turtle population dropped sharply. In 1890 alone, fisheries caught only 738 turtles along the entire length of the Indian River and

Completed about 1894, Sebastian's Florida East Coast Railway depot was the first of the large stations constructed in Indian River County. Later, the depot was moved, but burned before it could be rehabilitated and preserved.

This photograph depicts Vero's Florida East Coast Railway depot about 1918. Originally built on Commerce Avenue between Eighteenth and Nineteenth Streets, the building was relocated in the 1980s to its present Fourteenth Avenue site. The Indian River County Historical Society rehabilitated the depot, which houses its Exhibit Center. One of the county's oldest surviving buildings, the landmark is listed in the National Register of Historic Places.

five years later a mere 519. Turtle season ended in late February with the arrival of sawfish and sharks, which often destroyed the gill nets used to catch the turtles.

Fish wholesalers and shippers enjoyed only a brief interlude of competitive shipping rates in the mid-1890s when railroad and riverboat interests engaged in a pricing war. The competitive climate evaporated when the railroad won. Even as the steamboat business waned, however, interest remained high in developing inlets along the east coast. Among those arguing for inlet dredging were recreational boaters. The U.S. Army Corps of Engineers first examined the feasibility of an inlet at Sebastian in 1905. By then, commercial river traffic had almost wholly disappeared, although recreational boating had grown enormously. In 1918 alone, the Corps recorded 100,000 yachts cruising the Indian River, most of them carrying wealthy, vacationing northerners.

By 1898, the FEC had built small wood-frame depots at Roseland, Sebastian, Wabasso, Woodley, Gifford, and Vero. Most were little more than flag stations.

J.R. Parrott, then vice-president of the FEC, estimated in 1898 that the company maintained along its mainline forty passenger stations, sixty passenger flag stations, and one hundred freight flag stations. Many settlements languished because of inadequate facilities and residents complained endlessly about rates and service. F. Charles Gifford filed a formal complaint with the Florida Railroad Commission in 1903 regarding the deplorable condition of the Vero flag depot. Later that year, after intervention by the commission, the railroad did construct a new passenger station. The FEC expanded and improved the depot in 1916 and 1936. The Indian River County Historical Society purchased the building in 1983, moved it to a nearby site and converted it to the Society's headquarters. The Vero depot is one of the county's oldest buildings, a landmark listed in the National Register of Historic Places.

Like people elsewhere in America, Florida residents complained about excessive rate charges. The state legislature responded in 1897 by establishing the Florida Railroad Commission, which helped resolve some conflicts, often interceding between railroads, shippers, and citizens to determine the size and location of stations, shipping rates, placement of mainline and spur routes, and a host of other concerns. The public perceived the commission as essential to its welfare. Railroad leaders often regarded the agency as a nuisance, and sometimes simply ignored its rulings, which often led to court injunctions and litigation. The passenger trade between St. Augustine, West Palm Beach

Woodley, Quay & Winter Beach

The unincorporated community of Winter Beach experienced several changes in name between the 1890s and 1920s. Organized in March 1894 as Woodley, the original name was provided by settler J. T. Gray, who had owned a plantation in Georgia by the same name. The Woodley designation lasted until March 1902, when residents renamed the settlement Quay, in honor of U. S. Senator Matthew Quay. A conservative Republican from Pennsylvania, Quay maintained a seasonal home in St. Lucie Village, north of Fort Pierce. Quay was beloved by area settlers after he spearheaded a federal appropriation to improve the Indian River channel from Goat Creek to the Indian River Inlet. Although residents recognized his contribution with the renaming, the designation only survived until the Florida land boom of the 1920s, when the name Winter Beach was adopted. Quay property owners during the early twentieth century included nurseryman William Wigfield, who relocated there from the Orchid area, railroad section foreman Walter Bobo, A.B. Dennis, S.L. LeCour, N.B. Hamilton, and L. Swab. In 1904, Daniel C. Cox set up a general store in Quay. A native son of Taylor County, Florida, Cox planted citrus and, in 1918, won election to the St. Lucie County Board of Commissioners. Later, he opened retail stores in Wabasso and Vero Beach with his son, Wiley F. Cox.

and Miami accounted for 72 percent of the FEC's income in the late 1890s. Local freight shipments contributed little to the company's business. In 1898, Parrott regarded Fort Pierce as the "only small hamlet worth speaking of" between Melbourne and West Palm Beach. The pleas of growers for lower rates fell on deaf ears. Henry Flagler wrote in 1899 that "nothing competes with Fla. oranges but Fla. oranges,—an advance in rates always comes out of the pocket of the consumer."

The settlements along the Indian River between Sebastian and Fort Pierce experienced little growth during the first decade of the twentieth century. Vero could claim only a few small businesses, such as the fisheries and packing facilities operated by W.F. Anderson, W.J. Bass, I.D. Jandreau, and O. Roach. T.C. Bass and F. Charles Gifford maintained general stores and N.O. Penny tended his orange groves. The Bass family was part of the G.H. Bass & Company of Wilton, Maine, prominent shoe manufacturers. Vero's population climbed slowly, reaching two hundred in 1910.

Three older settlements, Toledo, Woodley, and Wabasso, lay north of Vero. Toledo was organized about 1893 by William Wigfield, a native of Pennsylvania. It stood west of the railroad tracks and north of Houston Creek, about four miles north of Vero. Ten years after Toledo's founding, Frank Ayers and William Brown were its largest property holders. Ayers had initially built a palmetto shack near the later site of the Gordon Motel in Vero. He eventually settled at Vero, where he cultivated beans and other vegetables. He also planted citrus groves at Orchid Island. His wife, Dallas, in addition to tending the family garden, sold mosquito fans she made from palm fronds. A native of Georgia, William Brown farmed a Toledo homestead. Wigfield operated a nursery business, selling and planting citrus rootstock to farmers. In December 1893, when thirty-two people lived at Toledo, Wigfield applied for a post office there.

Woodley, named for a Georgia plantation, was established in about 1894 by James T. Gray, a native of South Carolina who opened its first general store. The village lay about five miles north of Vero. Other early property owners included George Hamley, Elias Mattis, and J.A. Sexton. Zollie Cavender was named postmaster there in 1894 and continued to serve until 1899, when Louis Harris, who operated a country store, assumed the post. Later, in 1902, Minor S. Jones, Jr., son of a prominent Brevard County judge, was appointed postmaster. Jones owned forty acres and operated a general store and express agency at Woodley. He began as postmaster by changing the name of the Woodley village to Quay.

In the late 1880s, boat builder George Sears and George W. King moved into Lowanna, a settlement north of Vero that the railroad later renamed Wabasso. An interesting trail of mythology surrounds the founding and naming of the community. One early Vero Beach newspaper credited the naming of Wabasso in 1893 to FEC vice-president J.R. Parrott. Wabasso, the paper claimed, was selected by Parrott from poetry crafted by Henry Wadsworth Longfellow, who used the Native-American name Wabasso in his poem, *The Song of Hiawatha*. First published in 1855, *Hiawatha* enjoyed many editions and translations, some illustrated by famous artists, such as Frederick Remington. Longfellow translated Wabasso, one of many Native American names punctuating the romantic American classic, as both "rabbit" and "the North." New Deal writers asserted that Guale Indians from Ossabaw Island, near Savannah, Georgia, brought with them the name of their homeland, transposed into Wabasso, when they migrated to Florida's east coast in the eighteenth century. Another source attributed the name to early settler George Sears of Iowa. Florida historian Allen Morris believed that settlers from Ossabaw Island, Georgia, applied the transposed name to the Florida village in 1898.

Whatever the source for the community's name, it is clear that John R. Leatherman applied to the U.S. Department of the Treasury for a post office at Wabasso in March 1897 and served as the first postmaster of the village. Deeds and other legal instruments associated with Ossabaw Island fail to corroborate that Leatherman or any of the early land holders of Wabasso, Florida, ever held property on Ossabaw Island. Although several settlers of Wabasso were Georgians, none can be placed in Savannah. And so, it remains unclear who named the community and whether the Wabasso name came from the rabbit of Longfellow's *Hiawatha* or a transposition of Ossabaw Island, Georgia.

Notwithstanding such uncertainties, Wabasso celebrates a century-long heritage of continuous occupation. Eban True platted a small subdivision there in the 1890s and George King sold most of his holdings in 1896 to postmaster John Leatherman. Leatherman maintained a ten-acre homestead in the village until 1902, when he conveyed the real estate and buildings to E.E. Smith. Other early residents and property owners in Wabasso included Abraham Dennis, Samuel Harris, W.S. Snow, Sylvanus and Walter Kitching. The FEC maintained substantial landholdings along its riverfront into the early twentieth century.

Oslo, located several miles south of Vero, grew from Florida's east coast Scandinavian colony movement. Between 1895 and about 1910, through various associations and companies, Henry Flagler organized and promoted ethnic agricultural colonies. Handbills printed in Danish and Swedish and distributed aboard steamers and trains out of New York advertised the sale of large tracts of inexpensive land for growing fruits and vegetables. The flyers traded upon the promise of long growing seasons. Scandinavians, many of them recent immigrants then cultivating prairie lands in the upper Midwest, made their way to Florida and created scattered settlements of "colonies" along the southeast coast at Boynton, Hallandale, Linton, Modelo (later Dania), and White City. In the late 1890s, Swedes settled in Hallandale and Danes in Modelo and White City.

> ### William "Buck" Martin
>
> Born February 23, 1850, on an Illinois farm, William "Buck" Martin at the age of thirteen joined a wagon train headed for the western region and San Francisco. He never again saw his family, according to Arnold Helseth, who in an interview at the Indian River County Historical Society, told about one of the region's early settlers. Martin spent a number of years as an Indian trader in the west before heading for Florida, reaching the Sunshine State during the winter of the Great Freeze, 1894–1895. He lived in the woods, where he built a "shack" for himself, said Arnold Helseth, and he "lived off of the land." Recalled Helseth: "Old Buck taught me how to hunt rabbits." Martin died June 6, 1942.

Florida's Scandinavian colony movement began at Oslo. The first of the local immigrants were the Helseths, Norwegians who earlier had settled in Minnesota. Born in Norway in 1860, Ole O. Helseth immigrated to the United States in 1880 and in 1896 resettled south of Vero and named the village of Oslo for his native capital. His brother, John Helseth, had organized in 1895 a settlement at Viking (current-day Indrio). John Helseth, a pioneer in pineapple cultivation, encouraged O.O. Helseth to abandon his upper Midwestern farm for Florida. Within a few years of moving his family from Minnesota, Ole Helseth, a carpenter by trade, helped establish a post office and railroad flag stop at Oslo. A successful planter and businessman, O.O. Helseth helped incorporate the Oslo Pineapple & Citrus Growers Association, the Farmers Bank of Vero, and the Vero Bank & Trust Company. He also served on a local bridge authority, which supervised the financing and construction of the first Vero bridge, and he later served as president of the Indian River Farms Drainage District.

The settlement of Gifford, north of Vero, was organized in the mid-1890s. Enumerated in the 1900 census as a Woodley precinct, the Gifford community emerged as an African-American village. Georgia farmer William Brown brought his wife, Dulois, and eight children to Gifford in the 1890s. James T. Gray established a country store there and in 1904 opened Gray's "Plat of Gifford," offering nineteen building lots east of the railroad. Gifford's settlers consisted mainly of native southerners who were looking to make a new start. South Carolinian Will Jeffers and Alabaman Alvin Espy tilled small farms. Some residents were railroad section hands. Those who claimed Gifford as their home in 1910 included Solomon Bennett, Zachariah Blake, Benjamin Drake, James Green, James Jenkins, John McKinley, Frank Putnam, and Washington Williams. J.A. Kennedy, O.A. Morgan, and J.H. Robinson managed general stores and James Miller and T.R. Gerald preached the gospel. W.E. Geoffrey in 1916 offered two hundred lots for sale in a large subdivision east of the railroad..

African-Americans also settled in Sebastian and Wabasso. Mose and Mollie Hill of Virginia were among the earliest black settlers in Sebastian, arriving there in the 1890s. By 1910, a railroad section crew making repairs to bridges and the mainline resided in the village. African-Americans made their way to Wabasso primarily as laborers for James Dodge and Alfred B. Michael. Dodge recruited Mill Williams to manage his citrus groves. Michael employed seven men from the West Indies who were supervised by foreman Mac McWiggin to cultivate and harvest his citrus holdings. No African-American settlers were recorded on the barrier island or in Vero or Oslo in the first decade of the twentieth century.

The 1910 census counted about 1,100 people living on homesteads near the banks of the Indian River in present-day Indian River County. Only 126 people resided on Orchid Island, the barrier island. Sebastian, with 323 residents, remained the region's trading center. Quay contained 250 residents and Vero 102, trailed by Gifford, Oslo, Roseland, and Wabasso. The next ten years was to produce monumental changes as reclamation transformed the landscape and shifted settlement to the west and south of Sebastian. Vero stood poised to become the region's leading center of population and a new town with English origins, Fellsmere, enjoyed a brief reign as the largest town in the region.

Vero Beach's African Americans

New Deal writers recorded an early tale that the Gifford family of Vero had angered Henry Flagler by asking an exaggerated price for its land and that, in retaliation, the FEC established a nearby African-American settlement, naming it Gifford. The railroad then skirted the Gifford family's property and the town named Gifford became the Negro section of Vero Beach. The 1910 census schedules appear to support that tradition, since the Vero precincts that year recorded no African-American residents.

Chapter Four
Reclamation and Town Building, 1911-1919

Reclamation, the name given a state-sponsored program to drain wetlands and create land for agriculture, began to redraw the map of southeast Florida in the second decade of the new century. The idea first surfaced in 1850 when the U.S. Congress gave Florida title to its wetland areas, 10 million acres in all. Hamilton Disston proved the technical feasibility of reclamation when he dredged and drained Kissimmee River valley lands he purchased in 1884. Farming communities sprouted on the "reclaimed" land. Two decades later, in 1904, Governor William S. Jennings announced that his "first and chief duty in handling (these lands) was to have them drained and reclaimed." Jennings' successor, Napoleon Bonaparte Broward, sponsored land reclamation as a reform measure during his term as governor (1905-1909). Believing that reclamation held the keys to economic development, Broward encouraged prominent railroad and newspaper interests to promote the program.

In 1905, the Florida legislature set up administrative machinery to create drainage districts and levy taxes on property within each district to help fund the program. Dredges were ordered to dig drainage canals. After a fierce political battle, the dredges *Everglades* and *Okeechobee* were christened in Fort Lauderdale and began work in 1907. Despite challenges of every sort, the state's reclamation program was to endure for nearly twenty years, changing the face of southeast Florida, especially the Everglades.

Growth along Florida's east coast in the early part of the twentieth century occurred almost exclusively on reclaimed lands. Throughout the region, settlements hemmed in by wetlands and hampered by periodic flooding received thousands of acres suitable for occupation, construction, farming, and roads. To the consternation of conservationists, the program irreversibly damaged the environment, but offered land for new towns, encouraged growth, and brought civilization to a region previously characterized as wilderness.

Steam shovels with huge buckets dredged the wetlands in Indian River County. Most of the organizers of the Indian River Farms Company were from other parts of the country. Many immediately fell in love with the lush tropical environment. Depicted here about 1919 is a group of company officials and investors standing in one of the huge buckets.

The census bureau counted nearly twenty drainage districts in 1920 between Duval County and Dade County. State-sponsored activity centered on Broward, Dade, and Palm Beach counties. The largest private projects, however, were found near Fellsmere, Fort Pierce, and Vero. By 1909, 3,800 acres of wetlands had been drained throughout the state, a number that rose to 1.5 million acres in 1919. By then, over 160,000 acres of reclaimed lands in south Florida had been placed into production, creating an important agricultural region.

Two of Florida's largest private reclamation projects were found in present-day Indian River County. The two were directed by men of vision with vast experience in real estate development. Both men succeeded, to a degree, in achieving their dreams, and within two decades they transformed the region, converting inaccessible swampland into richly productive agricultural real estate.

Fellsmere, the state's largest privately-funded Progressive-era reclamation project, was the brainchild of E. Nelson Fell, a New Zealand engineer of British ancestry. Born in 1858, Fell was educated at England's Royal School of Mines and then in Heidelberg, Germany. He gained mining experience in Brazil and Colorado, before moving in the 1880s to Narcoossee, Florida, where he developed a sugarcane plantation and supervised drainage activities. He built a home and entered local politics, serving on the Osceola Board of County Commissioners between 1890 and 1896. He left Florida in July 1897 to join the Klondike gold rush. The following year, the family business moved him to Siberia to manage the Sparsky copper mines. He was joined there by his wife, Anne, who was driven from their Narcoossee home by floods and the great freeze. To educate their children, Marian and Olivia, the Fells selected schools on the Siberian steppes and private schools in the United States and France.

Upon retiring from the family business in 1907, E. Nelson Fell settled in Warrenton, Virginia. But he soon returned to Florida to organize the Fellsmere Farms Company, though he also devoted time to travel and writing. He published several articles in *Atlantic Monthly,* and in 1916 Duffield Press published his *Russian and Nomad: Tales of the Kirghiz Steppes,* which described Fell's experiences in Siberia. A wealthy world traveler, Fell maintained homes in England, New York, and Virginia. Ironically, in the Florida town named for him, he never built a house; instead, the family often stayed with Ernest Everett, resident manager of the Fellsmere Company.

Fell's Florida real estate ventures—Narcoossee in the 1880s and Fellsmere in 1910—were associated with Florida's English colony movement. British investors and London land agents had become excited during the 1880s about the potential for creating fortunes in growing Florida citrus. Central Florida especially became a popular site for immigrants, who settled Acton and Lakeland in Polk County, Conway and Orlando in Orange County, and Narcoossee in Osceola County. The great freeze of 1895 cost many of those English settlers their investments. Most either returned to England or moved farther south into the Florida peninsula. Fell's first venture, Narcoossee, fit that pattern. His second Florida development scheme, Fellsmere, did not specifically target English settlers. He reached out to Americans as well.

Beginning in 1910, the Fellsmere Farm Company acquired 118,000 acres of muck, prairie, and pine lands, located nine miles west of the St. Sebastian River, that it set about to drain and develop. With a capital stock of $2 million, the company consisted initially of three stockholders. Oscar Crosby served as president and E. Nelson Fell as vice president. The board of directors included bankers, lawyers, engineers, and a railroad specialist, primarily from the Northeast. A local newspaper, *Fellsmere Farmer,* began publication in 1911 and the settlement acquired a post office, an electric plant and a rail connection between the Fellsmere Farms Railroad and the FEC line at Sebastian. Operating with one locomotive and several cars, the railroad brought settlers, construction materials, and dredges to the area and transported produce and crops to market. Dredges cut canals, providing irrigation and drainage to farm lands. The main canal control gate was completed in June 1913, affording settlers a degree of protection from periodic floods.

In July 1911, the company cut out a small portion of its tract for the town of Fellsmere. The nearly one square mile town plan consisted of an orthogonal ten-block grid with parks, diagonal streets, a broad circular intersection, and divided boulevards. East-west avenues displayed the names of various states of the Union; north-south streets the names of

These Fellsmere landmarks, all listed in the National Register of Historic Places, were built at the height of the city's historic development. At the top is the Marian Fell Library, completed in April 1915 with the aid of publication royalties donated by the daughter of city founder E. Nelson Fell. In the center is the 1915 Fellsmere School, one of the region's largest public projects of that era. At the bottom is the First Methodist Episcopal Church. The congregation was organized in 1914 and built its sanctuary on Broadway in 1924.

Fellsmere had blossomed into St. Lucie County's second largest town when a photographer snapped this image about 1914. Facing north on Broadway just north of the intersection of New York Avenue, the picture depicts the Fellsmere Railroad depot in the distance and commercial stores along the main street in town. The Hale & Brown Building at the left was constructed in 1913; the Fellsmere Community Club appears at the far right. Demolition and fire later consumed most of the buildings pictured here.

citrus, hardwood, and conifer trees. The ambitious Fellsmere town plan reflected planning concepts associated with the City Beautiful movement that influenced urban design early in the century.

To compete for land sales and settlers with the developers of nearby Fort Pierce Farms and Indian River Farms in Vero, the Fellsmere board of directors launched an ambitious public relations campaign throughout the eastern half of the United States. The company used an underwriting agency in Chattanooga, Tennessee as its sales agent and also maintained offices in Jacksonville, then the gateway city of Florida. Circulars touted inexpensive land and the opportunity for agricultural fortune. A ten-acre "demonstration farm" exhibited the assortment of crops that might be grown on the land, including eggplant, figs, oranges, persimmons, strawberries, and sugarcane. Resident manager Ernest Everett built a platform over the smokestacks of the dredge *St. Lucie,* giving prospective buyers an unparalleled view of the landscape from forty feet above the ground.

Within two years of its founding, the Fellsmere Farms Company claimed to have drained 8,000 acres of wetlands. The early success of its demonstration farm encouraged the developers to portray the town as an agricultural wonderland with unlimited potential. In its first year, the farm produced celery worth $2,500 per acre. It claimed that sweet potatoes, costing $5 per acre to raise, brought as much as $350 at market. The farm also produced tomatoes, cucumbers, peanuts, corn, and squash, and promoted raising spices and nuts, including macadamia nuts, cinnamon ginger roots, and Japanese persimmons.

Fruit became an important cash crop. Fellsmere promoters claimed that a grapefruit tree that cost $6.50 to plant with proper maintenance in five years would yield $50 annually. Oranges also furnished a substantial income. One planter reported that the harvest from a twelve-acre grove yielded $7,000. The company claimed investors had planted 750 acres of orange trees by 1916. It appeared that virtually any tree or plant flourished in Fellsmere muck. In the western fringe of the development 2,000 acres were reserved for sugarcane cultivation. Cotton, cattle, poultry, and bees were also found on farms at Fellsmere. Land cost $55 per acre. Terms included one-third down and a ten-acre minimum investment.

Henry Adams and E. Nelson Fell

The Fell family's national circle of friends prominently included Henry Adams, a renowned Harvard University historian and author and descendant of two presidents. Adams often corresponded with the Fells, especially Anne. Earlier, in 1897, while Anne still resided in Narcoossee, Adams lamented his circumstances in Paris and the condition of the city, musing that "Paris is like Purgatory, a place where all rubbish of human nature drifts, because the Almighty does not know what else to do with it." Incredibly, while there he longed for the serenity of central Florida (which he had never visited), ruminating that "...but I think you have the best of it, and that the peace of Narcoossee is better than the business of London and Paris.... Is not this a cool-gray landscape? Doesn't it make Narcoossee seem rich and purple? Certainly I should not be half as solitary in Narcoossee as I am in Paris." Adams' long association with Charles Scribner's & Sons helped influence the publishing house to review and publish E. Nelson Fell's articles on life in Russia. Adams tried but failed in 1917 to secure a diplomatic assignment in Russia for E. Nelson Fell.

Within the town of Fellsmere itself, carpenters assembled eighteen residences in 1911 and thirty-six dwellings in 1912, along with three stores. The population reached 503 in 1913, making Fellsmere the second largest town in St. Lucie County, second only to Fort Pierce in size. The Fellsmere Bank, incorporated with $25,000, opened in July 1913. The Dixie Playhouse was built on Broadway and G.F. Green, D. Howard Saunders, and Stuart R. Greiner organized the Fellsmere Realty Company. The Union Church was established in 1913. A divided concrete-paved boulevard, Broadway was one of the first hard-surfaced roads in St. Lucie County. Sheriff Dan Carleton of Fort Pierce predicted Fellsmere would become the largest town in the county within a few years.

Fellsmere incorporated in May 1915, the first municipal government within present-day Indian River County. C.W. Talmadge, G.F. Green, and Wallace Sherwood were elected councilmen and moved at once to begin installing additional paved streets, sidewalks, street lighting, and electrical service. In 1915, E. Nelson Fell helped organize a producer's exchange, which packed and shipped

Typical of houses built in Fellsmere about 1915 are those pictured to the right. The home and office of the Fellsmere Company surveyor appears in the upper photograph, and the Elder House below it. Among the oldest buildings in Fellsmere is the Fellsmere Inn at 107 North Broadway, pictured at the bottom. Built about 1910 by the Fellsmere Farms Company, the inn served as the city's social center for several decades. In 1913, the company sold the building to Theodore Moore, a Miami businessman. A native of North Carolina, Moore moved to Dade County in 1902, where he developed pineapple fields and citrus groves. Known as Florida's "Pineapple King," Moore also cultivated pineapple fields in Fellsmere. About 1915, the hotel was renamed the Broadway Inn, probably by Moore, a name it retained into the 1930s. The arrival of the hotel on Broadway marked that street as the commercial center of Fellsmere.

fruits and vegetables. A farmer's loan association assisted growers with financing the purchase of land, rootstock, and seed for groves and fields. A progressive thinker, Fell brought his ideals to city government. The city charter gave women the right to vote, the first municipality in Florida to do so, an act that has been called the legislative beginnings of the suffrage movement in Florida.

Fellsmere's African-American community dates to the arrival of the Fellsmere Farms Company, which hired black laborers to help construct the railroad and cook for the survey crew that laid out the development. Black settlers developed a neighborhood near the northeast corner of the town plan bounded by the railroad and Willow and Booker streets. J.G. Carter, R.L. James, and Murray Hall, Fellsmere merchants and community leaders, sold lots to settlers. Children began attending a school in 1913, where they were instructed by B.F. James. Churches played an important part in local culture. The Missionary Baptist Church, organized by Reverend Calloway in 1911, constructed a sanctuary in 1915. After fire destroyed the building in 1920, another was completed in 1923. A second church, the Church of God in Christ, was organized in 1919 and a third, the Bethel A.M.E. congregation, in 1925.

Ernest Barnwell

Born in 1910 into a family of former slaves, Ernest Barnwell moved from Jacksonville to the Indian River region with his mother. There, he attended school until the ninth grade, no mean accomplishment for a black youth at that time, before beginning work as a farmer. He worked on the bean and tomato farms of several large landowners, among them J. O. Edwards and Robert T. Crocker. He remembers especially the swarming mosquitoes in the fields. "You couldn't hold a conversation with anyone on the farm unless you were wearing a mesh veil to protect you against the insects," he said. Several farms that he worked were located on the peninsula. There was no bridge across the Indian River at the time, so the workers took a barge across the water on Monday and did not return until Saturday. Ernest recalled in an interview recorded at the Indian River County Historical Society that his brother, Clifford, was the "first colored man from Indian River County to be killed in World War II."

Growth also spurred the county school board to replace the original school, a small wood frame building built in 1911. The board issued bonds to finance construction of a two-story, $40,000 masonry building designed by architect Frederick H. Trimble. A native of Canada, Trimble served as an architect for the Methodist Episcopal Church in China before relocating to Fellsmere and, in 1916, to Orlando. He designed about fifty public schools in Florida, in addition to a campus plan and several buildings on the Florida Southern College campus in Lakeland. He returned to the Indian River region in

This 1911 promotional map depicts the scale of the Fellsmere Farms Company reclamation and development project.

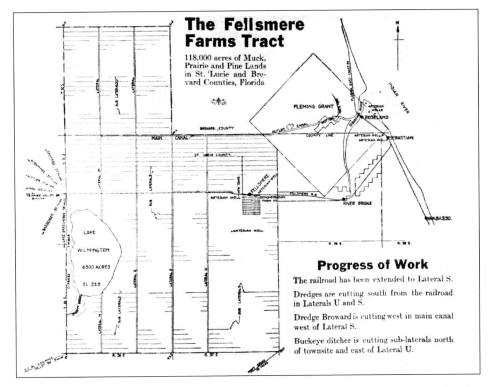

The Fellsmere Farms Tract

118,000 acres of Muck, Prairie and Pine Lands in St. Lucie and Brevard Counties, Florida

Progress of Work

The railroad has been extended to Lateral S.

Dredges are cutting south from the railroad in Laterals U and S.

Dredge Broward is cutting west in main canal west of Lateral S.

Buckeye ditcher is cutting sub-laterals north of townsite and east of Lateral U.

the 1920s to draw plans for the Vero Theater and Royal Park Inn in Vero Beach. The Fellsmere Public School, completed in 1916, was Trimble's first public project in Florida and the largest building constructed in Fellsmere during its early development.

The completion of the school marked the peak of Fellsmere's growth. An unusually heavy rainfall in July 1915, thirteen inches of rain in twenty-four hours, overwhelmed the drainage system and flooded the area. The high water killed nearly 5,000 citrus trees and resulted in a dearth of production that year. Some residents fled to better drained areas in south Florida and along the coast, including the nearby towns of Fort Pierce, Melbourne, and Vero, all of which occupied higher ground.

The poor sales contributed to the unraveling of E. Nelson Fell's dreams in the next year. The company had spent $1 million reclaiming wetlands and it needed steady income from lot sales and agricultural production. Failing to meet its obligations, the Fellsmere Farms Company filed for bankruptcy. In 1918, the successor Fellsmere Company acquired the mortgage, holdings, and railroad of the defunct Fellsmere Farms Company for $350,000. E. Nelson Fell retired to his Virginia estate. His association with the company ended in 1917. He never returned to

Fellsmere and died in 1928. The population of Fellsmere, 503 strong in 1913, dropped to 333 in 1920.

South of Fellsmere, the Indian River Farms Company was organized at Vero. Capitalized in September 1912 with $1 million, the corporation was backed largely by Iowa investors. The company initially purchased 48,000 acres, an area about one-half the size of the Fellsmere reclamation project. Indian River Farms was, as events proved, better organized than its northern competitor. J.H. Hass served as the first president of the company, but Herman J. Zeuch was its organizing genius. The Indian River Farms, like the Fellsmere Farms Company, focused on selling reclaimed land, which it peddled through sales offices in Vero, Davenport, Iowa and Colorado Springs, Colorado. It drew up a drainage plan in 1913 that provided for a main outlet canal emptying into the Indian River immediately north of Vero. The flood that deluged Fellsmere caused few problems for Vero settlers. The first phase of excavation was essentially complete by 1917. Successfully promoted, the company sold former wetlands to citrus companies, land speculators, developers, and wealthy seasonal residents seeking a Florida estate.

A native of Iowa, Herman J. Zeuch organized the Indian River Farms Company at Vero. His vision of the region included developing a picturesque town plan with boulevards and parks "with an eye single to modern improvements."

The rich soils and scenic vistas along the Indian River captivated Zeuch. Many of Zeuch's friends and associates in Iowa believed reclaiming Florida wetlands constituted a far greater risk than developing land in the Northwest Territories. After engaging several surveying and engineering companies to estimate the costs for reclaiming the land, Zeuch settled on civil engineer William H. Kimball of Iowa, who had previously worked on railroad projects. With assistant Robert D. Carter, Kimball developed a feasible plan for draining the back country. Carter arrived in Vero in January 1912 with a crew of twelve men, a wagon and team, and two large tents. As part of the development scheme, the company laid out the Town of Vero in 1914. Zeuch instructed Kimball and Carter to organize a picturesque town plan with boulevards and parks "with an eye single to modern development and improvement."

Intrigued by Indians, Zeuch selected Native American names for streets. About 1912, the company hired J. Hudson Baker, a newly-arrived builder from Missouri, to construct a hotel to accommodate visitors. Zeuch named it after Chief

An Indian River Farms Company drag-line excavator dredges a drainage canal near Vero's municipal water works. By April 1920, the company had dredged 162 miles of main, lateral, and sublateral canals. At the time, it owned three dredges, including one floating excavator.

Sleepy Eye of Minnesota, and recounted years later a folk tale that the chief had boasted "he never spilt a drop of blood of the white man." Zeuch expressed "regret and disappointment" when in the early 1930s the streets were renamed. Although the Giffords had actually first settled Vero, Zeuch claimed it as his creation. His biographical sketch in the 1930 *Who's Who in America* described Zeuch as the "Builder of towns of Taber, Alberta, Can. and Vero Beach, Fla."

Still, Zeuch generously praised his associates, James E. Andrews, Arthur M. Hill, Dr. John L. Hutchison, Eli C. Walker, Anthony W. Young, and others, for the success of Vero and Indian River Farms. In fifteen years, the company expended $1,349,000 for drainage, road building, and surveying and dredged nearly four hundred miles of canals. Those activities had just begun to encourage settlement and building construction when World War I began. Zeuch recalled in the 1930s that but for the war "we would probably have a town now of from ten to fifteen thousand people, instead of the village of twenty six to twenty seven hundred . . . ."

E. Nelson Fell and Herman Zeuch met in 1914 to inspect each other's projects and to discuss drainage and reclamation. Recalling the meeting many years later, Zeuch said that he had expressed doubt about Fell's drainage plans. Fell responded, "Why my dear Mr. Zeuch, this thing has all been figured out on a scientific basis; we know the rainfall, we know just what the carry off capacity of our ditches is, and we figured this thing out to the last gallon." Zeuch said he then yielded to what he thought was Fell's better professional judgement. No two men better represent the hopes and fears, the success and failure, the triumph and the tragedy of land development in Florida than E. Nelson Fell and Herman Zeuch.

Within a year of the exchange, storm waters had nearly washed away Fellsmere. As Zeuch had predicted, the drainage system proved far less efficient than Fell had estimated. One Fellsmere Farm official later admitted that Broadway Avenue, with its poured concrete street and molded curbs and gutters, often became with passing storms "miniature Venetian Canals." Even half a decade after the flood, tourists asking residents for directions to Fellsmere as they traveled the Dixie Highway were often advised that the town was "knee deep in water." Fell abandoned the city named for him.

The Sleepy-Eye Lodge was among the first buildings constructed by the Indian River Farms Company in Vero. Herman J. Zeuch named the hostelry after Chief Sleepy Eye of Minnesota, recalling that the chief had boasted "he never spilt a drop of blood of the white man." Located at the southwest corner of Fourteenth Avenue and Twenty-First Street, the Sleepy Eye Lodge was moved in February 1925 to make room for the new Hotel Vero Del Mar. Relocated to Twenty-Second Street and Nineteenth Avenue, the lodge was renamed the Hotel Del Prado.

Indian River Farms redoubled its excavation efforts in the wake of the Fellsmere flood. By 1917, when the company completed the first phase of the project, it excavated over 2 million cubic yards of muck and built a six-mile main canal, thirty-six miles of lateral canals, twenty-six miles of dikes, and one hundred twenty miles of sublateral canals. The Florida Legislature provided for a Vero Drainage District, which was reorganized into the Indian River Farms Drainage District in May 1919. The district assessed a uniform tax of 40 cents per acre to conduct additional drainage. A plan for additional reclamation in 1920 raised $576,000 to improve main canals, dredge new laterals, and construct highway bridges over the canals.

Even early settlers who preceded the Indian River Farms credited the company for their later success. Louis Harris left Gainesville for Johns Island in the 1890s, where he worked as postmaster and an agent for the Indian River Steamboat Company. In 1906, after the steamboat business evaporated, he resettled south of Vero and began growing citrus and fruits. Heavily invested in real estate, Harris helped organize the Vero Land Company about 1910 and the Farmer's Bank of Vero in 1914. By 1920, he was president of the bank. Harris also helped organize the Vero Fruit Growers Association. The editors of the *Vero Press* were impressed with his "elegant six-room bungalow, which adds greatly to the beauty of this section." He later served on the school boards of St. Lucie and Indian River Counties and eventually worked as superintendent of schools for Indian River County.

Eli C. Walker, a native of Georgia, lived for a time in Woodley-Quay upon arrival in Florida in 1906. Walker purchased the Headgrove and was producing citrus when the Indian River Farms Company acquired the surrounding property and initiated its drainage plan. Zeuch obviously thought highly of him. In the early 1920s Walker's ten-acre grove annually produced about 5,000 boxes of citrus, producing an annual income of $10,000. Most of his grove workers were African Americans, for whom he supplied tenant housing and some of whom labored for Walker for several decades. The native Georgian invested in various Vero businesses, including the Farmers Bank of Vero, Vero Bank & Trust Company, and the Seminole Building Corporation. In the mid-1930s, Walker served in the Florida legislature.

Brothers C.M. and L.H. Vinnedge of Anderson, Indiana, and St. Louis, Missouri, respectively, pooled their resources in developing the Vinnedge Farms Company of Florida. Successful mid-western businessmen, the Vinnedge brothers first visited Vero in March 1917. C.M. Vinnedge operated an insurance business in Indiana and L.H. Vinnedge served as vice-president of the Atlas Crucible Steel Corporation of New York. The pair purchased a sixty-acre tract of prairie astride the main drainage canal and, soon, another forty-five acres. Within two years, their company had planted nearly 7,000 citrus trees, including Duncan, Lue Gim Gong, and Parson Brown varieties, on ninety-five acres. Wind breaks planted with bamboo divided the groves into twenty-acre tracts. Anticipating expansion of the business, the company, in 1921, doubled the capital stock to $200,000, making shares available to investors in Chicago, Cleveland, New York, and St. Louis.

Most citrus varieties planted by Indian River farmers had been introduced by farmers and horticulturists in the nineteenth century. Generally, a variety was identified either by the name of its propagator, its first substantial planter, or, in some cases, the region in which it was planted. Nurseries offered a variety of oranges, each displaying unique characteristics and maturing in slightly different seasons. The Dummitt, one of the oldest varieties along the Indian River, traces

Peggy Cole Faircloth

Peggy Cole Faircloth was living in Illinois with her grandmother when her mother moved to Vero in 1917. She recalls her mother's description of the new place as "wild and exotic," filled with "swamps, snakes, and too many mosquitoes." Her two uncles, Harvey and Hershel, saw a need for a plumbing service in the growing community and organized Moore Plumbing and Construction. They knew little of plumbing when they began, she recalled in a 1988 interview, but went door to door installing outhouses and septic tanks and "eventually became pretty good at their trade."

its ancestry to the budwood of Spanish, wild, sweet orange trees obtained from Port Orange and planted on Merritt Island by Douglas Dummitt about 1830. Edward H. Hart introduced Hart's Late Valencia at Federal Point on the St. Johns River in 1867. The Parson Brown variety, first planted in large groves near Lake Weir, originated in the grove of the Reverend Nathan Brown of Webster in 1878. In 1879, Judge Isaac Stone planted his Glenwood grove with a variety he named Hamlin for a DeLand friend and attorney. The Hamlin was the principal orange cultivated in Florida during the nineteenth century. Chinese immigrant Lue Gim Gong introduced a new variety in DeLand by crossing the Mediterranean Sweet with Hart's Late in 1886. His experiment led the American Pomological Society to award Lue Gim Gong its prestigious Wilder Medal in 1911.

Facing south along Twenty-First Street in May 1916, a photographer recorded the dedication ceremonies for the Unity Club, the original name given the Vero Beach Woman's Club. A decade after its founding, the club boasted a membership of 125 and, in January 1927, dedicated a new addition to the clubhouse. Now listed in the National Register of Historic Places, the Vero Beach Woman's Club played an important role in Indian River County's social history. In the distance stands the original Vero Baptist Church, also built in 1916.

Many farmers also planted grapefruit, at the time widely known as "pomelos," from the Dutch word "pompelmoes." Florida farmers began exporting grapefruit in the 1880s. Indian River planters preferred the Duncan and Marsh varieties. A.L. Duncan first cultivated the Duncan near Dunedin in the 1890s. C.M. Marsh introduced his variety in Lakeland in 1895. The tree from which Marsh started the variety was reportedly then sixty years old, having survived pests and freezes. John Thompson's DeSoto variety came out of Clearwater in 1895, and the Standard, a native of the Indian River region, came from Rockledge about 1886. With fanciful advertisements and colorful catalogs, nurseries began at the turn-of-the-century merchandising those varieties. Typical of the larger Florida companies were G.L. Taber's Glen St. Mary Nurseries and A. R. Klemm's Winter Haven Nurseries. Indian River planters often relied on such companies for rootstock and other nursery needs. Articles in farm journals, such as the *Florida Agriculturist* of DeLand and Jacksonville's *Florida Dispatch,* contained information about plant pests, irrigation, and methods to increase crop yields.

Zeuch's enterprise succeeded and the community grew. The First Methodist congregation, organized in April 1914, completed a wood-frame sanctuary in 1917. The Baptists constructed a church building in April 1915. Both congregations held services in the Vero school until the completion of their respective buildings. Lutherans initially gathered at the home of Hans Clemann on Forty-third Avenue and then held services at the Harris School until 1919, when a sanctuary was completed one block west of the Baptist church. That same year, parishioners of St. Helen's Catholic built their church.

Physician David Rose arrived in Sebastian in 1908. A graduate of Toronto University, Rose had practiced medicine for twenty-four years in Canada and Chicago before retiring to Florida. Initially, he planted citrus, but residents prevailed upon him to resume his professional practice. Soon, he was traveling by horse-and-carriage between Melbourne and Fort Pierce to treat patients. He also established a contract with the FEC to serve as a company surgeon. Between 1925 and 1929 alone, Rose recorded nearly 5,000 house calls in his medical journal. An honorary member of the Florida State Medical Society, Rose later served several terms on the county school board.

In 1916, Jacksonville banking barons Bion H. Barnett and William D. Barnett, in association with former Florida Gov. Francis P. Fleming, organized the Sebastian Ranch Company to "buy, own, and sell and use for breeding purposes horses, cattle, sheep, hogs, and other livestock." Another enterprise, the Sebastian Land Company, initiated timber and naval stores operations near Sebastian in 1919. Company organizers H.W. Mercer and W.F. Graves had gained their timbering experience in west Florida forests near Cottondale and DeFuniak Springs.

The extraction of turpentine from pine forests near Wabasso and Sebastian contributed to Florida's naval stores industry, which accounted for 30 percent of the nation's production in 1900. Turpentine camps varied in size. Most consisted of a still, spirit shed, rosin yard, blacksmithery, cooperage shed, cup-cleaning vat, barn and wagon shed, and living quarters for the manager and workers. Camps generally stood within a forest owned or leased by a company to facilitate moving sap to the still. A "woods rider" marked suitable trees with an axe, smoothing the bark several feet above the ground. A "chipper" hewed slashes about one inch deep into each tree, about four feet above the roots. Metal gutters and clay or galvanized iron cups were attached to the tree below this "face." The cups filled with resinous sap and about once a month were emptied, or "dipped," into metal buckets that, in turn, were poured

---

Bernice Meyer

Bernice Meyer traveled with her sister from Davenport, Iowa to Vero, arriving in 1915 to a land she thought was "roses and sunshine." To plant his orange grove, her father had first to clear the land. They lived out on "Rosewood Avenue, 16th Street," she recalled in an interview nearly three quarters of a century later. The family home was located about three miles from downtown Vero, a distance she often traveled by wagon, returning with a block of ice. Her father, said Bernice Meyer, built the First Methodist Church.

into fifty-five gallon barrels. Chippers gradually lengthened the face on each tree to extract more sap, essentially bleeding the tree to death. After a tree yielded most of its sap, it was felled for its lumber.

At Wabasso and Orchid, the Deerfield Groves Company brought powerful Florida and Pennsylvania marketing interests to the Indian River region. Organized as a New Jersey corporation in June 1912, the company used a trademark name belonging to Edward Porcher, a Cocoa banker, planter, and marketing expert. Porcher, who had settled in Merritt Island in 1884 and helped form the Indian River Orange Grower's Association and Lake Worth Pineapple

---

Anne Gollnick Keen

Married in Missouri in 1915, the parents of Anne Keen, Leon S. Gollnick and Lillie Robertson, immediately left for Florida, bringing even horses and cows in an "immigrant train." The house they settled in was surrounded by water, Anne Keen remembers, and soon "they started digging the small canal in front of the house. It was all done by hand." Leon Gollnick began raising cabbage, beans, and potatoes, graduating in time to citrus and eventually expanding to 100 acres of groves. He belonged to the "Old Vero Indian River Producers Association," which, Anne Keen recalls, "took care of everything from the grove to the market."

Organized as the A. Livingston Mission of the Methodist Conference, the Grace Methodist Episcopal Church of Wabasso constructed this sanctuary in 1917. The edifice, which stands at 8799 Fiftieth Avenue, was later renamed Grace United Methodist Church.

Vero's Baptists met in April 1915 and, in 1916, completed a house of worship (above). Substantial growth prompted the congregation to build a larger sanctuary capable of seating 500. Completed at a cost of $14,000, the new building, pictured below it, was dedicated in 1936.

Roach's Vero Garage occupied a prominent site in Vero at the southeast corner of Dixie Highway and Twentieth Street. Completed in 1912, the building employed wood frame walls covered by pressed metal panels that looked like rough-faced concrete blocks.

Grower's Association in the 1890s, recognized the savings generated through association with other growers. Aware that a distinctive label and name would encourage repeat sales, he marked fruit from his own groves with the trademark "Deerfield Groves." He constructed a packing house, planted still more groves, and by the mid-1930s owned 350 acres of citrus on Merritt Island.

Porcher's early partner, James Crutchfield, left Florida in 1896 and formed with Robert Woolfolk a commission wholesale company, Crutchfield & Woolfolk, headquartered in Pittsburg, Pennsylvania. In 1919, Crutchfield & Woolfolk was reorganized into American Fruit Growers, Inc. AFG, as it was commonly known, became a national fruit and vegetable marketing organization. The company's distinctive "Blue Goose" label gained national recognition. Frank Skelly managed the local office in Orlando, already a banking and citrus center. By 1921, three packing houses in Vero were affiliated with AFG.

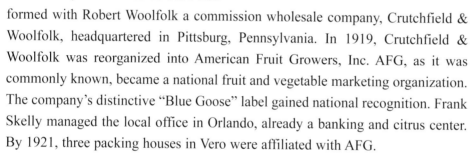

Crutchfield and Porcher believed the Deerfield Groves label could be used to dominate sales of Indian River citrus. Initially, Deerfield Groves shipped its harvest from Orchid by boat to Cocoa, where Porcher's packing house prepared the fruit for shipment. In 1916 the company harvested 19,000 boxes of citrus. Two years later, it earned a profit of nearly $60,000. To reduce the cost of shipping the fruit from Orchid to Cocoa, the company built a packing house at Wabasso.

Crutchfield and Porcher parted company in 1920. Crutchfield remained with Deerfield Groves, which retained the corporate name, but adopted other label names, such as Flint, Indian Deer, Orchid, and AFG's Blue Goose label. Crutchfield's business partner, Robert Woolfolk, was elected president of Deerfield Groves. Alfred B. Michael, a local businessman, became vice president. Michael's father, S.K. Michael, a native of West Virginia, had moved the family to Indian River Narrows in 1887, where Alfred attended school. After graduating from college in Macon, Georgia, Alfred operated a schooner on the Indian River and then opened a general store in Eden, Florida before returning to Orchid in

Wabasso, as it looked in about the year 1914. Facing the Indian River, this scene depicts E.E. Smith's general store on the right. Residences to the left of the road, from the nearest to the most distant, are the Eby House, Sam Beer House, E.E. Smith House, George Sears House, and Tom Cail House. Sisby Scruggs, then a teacher at Wabasso Elementary, reportedly climbed a nearby tree to snap this photograph. Scruggs later attended the University of Florida Law School and became a prominent Gainesville attorney.

Beverly Michael Graves

Stephen Michael brought his wife and eight children with him from Pawpaw, West Virginia when he moved to Vero in 1897. For a time in the early part of the new century the family lived elsewhere in Florida, but returned to the Indian River region in 1918, settling then at Orchid. Beverly Michael, who returned with her parents in 1918, recalls the latter move. The family moved into a house that was once a post office and before that a one-room school house. Before the Wabasso bridge spanning the Indian River was built, Beverly remembers having to take a boat to the mainland to buy basic items such as sugar and flour. When the family was not able to get into town, they would wait at the river for a boat that brought supplies from Jacksonville once a month.

These photographs on this page depict residences belonging to two generations of the Michael family. The house above was built by S. K. Michael following his arrival in 1887. The Mediterranean residence to the right was the home of his son, Alfred B. Michael, who played a prominent role in organizing Florida's citrus industry.

1901. He planted a grove on the peninsula and in 1917 consolidated his holdings with those of the Deerfield Groves Company.

The company prospered under Michael's direction. A daily average of twelve rail cars filled with fruit left the Wabasso packing house during the 1921-1922 season. The company expanded its holdings at Orchid and purchased half interest in the Graves Brothers vegetable packing house at Wabasso. In the 1930s, Michael helped organize the Indian River Citrus League, which obtained a ruling by the Federal Trade Commission prohibiting marketers from applying the Indian River designation to fruit grown outside the region. Deerfield Groves Company later developed the trade names Acme, Flint, Indian Deer, Loveland, Orchid, and Orkideer to market its Indian River fruit and build customer loyalty. Michael's reputation in the industry advanced and in 1948 he became president of the Florida Citrus Mutual in Lakeland.

Encouraged by the progress of reclamation and bumper harvests, the FEC constructed a branch line through the Kissimmee River Valley to Lake Okeechobee. Railroad lines built deep into the interior by the Atlantic Coast Line and Seaboard Air Line companies compelled the FEC to secure its hold on inland areas of Florida's east coast. Way stations with Seminole names such as Bithlo, Holopaw, Nittaw, Pocataw, Osowaw, and Wewahotee sprang up between New Smyrna and Lake Okeechobee. Most survived only briefly as saw mill villages. By 1915, the 122-mile line reached the south shore of Lake

The Robert D. Carter Family

For most of the twentieth century, three generations of the Carter family helped guide the growth and development of Vero Beach and Indian River County. A civil engineer, Robert D. Carter arrived in 1911 to work on drainage for the Indian River Farms Company. He directed the initial survey for Vero Beach, laid out Royal Park, and in 1926 surveyed the route for State Road 60. Following Robert's death in 1956, his son, Egerton E. Carter, assumed the presidency of the R. D. Carter Engineering firm. Egerton's son, Marvin E. Carter, a registered surveyor, joined the company in 1962.

Ed Carter's daughter, Mildred "Millie" Carter Frasier Bunnell, devoted much of her life to improving the community. Active in the local Bicentennial celebration, she served as one of the first presidents of the Indian River County Historical Society. Millie rallied support to preserve the Vero Beach Community Center. The restored building, named the Heritage Center, now contains a small museum dedicated to Indian River citrus. Before her untimely death in the spring of 2000, Millie formed Indian River County's first storytelling group, gathering oral accounts of local history. "Millie's ideas, her energy, and her encouragement will be missed, but her legacy will always be with us," said Ruth Stanbridge, County Commissioner and County Historian, in her eulogy to one of the county's most beloved citizens.

Okeechobee, running through an area that later became Indian River County. At the time, only about 6,200 people inhabited the widely scattered settlements along the line between southeast Volusia County and western Palm Beach County.

Thirty miles west of Vero, near Blue Cypress Lake, originally named Lake Wilmington, the railroad cut across the southwestern tip of the present-day county. There the FEC established the village of Yeehaw, a corruption of the Seminole word *yaha,* translated as "wolf." Various railroad companies held title to land in the vicinity in the 1890s. In 1910, the Southern States Land & Timber Company acquired 70,000 acres in western St. Lucie County. Later, the Consolidated Land Company of Jacksonville, Florida purchased acreage in the same region. Excitement arose in 1913 when the dredge *St. Lucie* emerged from the Fellsmere mucklands into the crystal-clear waters of Blue Cypress Lake. Intended to drain the wetlands, the man-made canal also supported the movement of launches that carried sightseers and fishermen from Fellsmere and towns along the coast into the backcountry.

The FEC built a small depot at Yeehaw about 1915. The Consolidated Land Company pursued forest operations in the area until about 1925, when State Road 60, an east-west road, entered the settlement. Scholars working for the Works Progress Administration (WPA) during the Great Depression of the 1930s recorded several scattered dwellings, a filling station, a general store, and eight inhabitants at Yeehaw. The original Yeehaw community disappeared after World War II and was replaced by Yeehaw Junction, which assumed the old Seminole name at a new location west of the county line on U.S. Highway 441 near Florida's Turnpike.

As war engulfed Europe in 1914, Americans looked on apprehensively, hoping against hope during the next three years that they might avoid the expanding conflict. Despite the promises of President Woodrow Wilson, the United States joined England and France in 1917, closing the curtain on an exhausted Turn-of-the-Century Era and silencing the faded echoes of the Victorian Age. Agricultural production and sales profited from the war, but the national mobilization effort consumed building materials and construction workers. Development activities sputtered to a halt. Still, the progress of reclamation and agricultural development of the century's early years had set an inviting example. When, after eighteen months of war, peace returned, Americans were more than eager to resume their exploitation of raw lands and the building of cities and towns. An era of explosive growth ensued.

Chapter Five
Boom and Bust, 1919-1928

THE END OF WORLD WAR I LAUNCHED AN ERA OF UNRIVALED ECONOMIC EXPANSION in Florida. The state's population rose from 968,470 to 1,468,21. Thirteen new counties, including Indian River County, were organized. Improved transportation networks facilitated travel by automobile and railroad. By mid-decade, 6,000 miles of railroad tracks and 1,600 miles of roadways crisscrossed the state. Twenty-five passenger trains arrived daily in Jacksonville, bringing over 600,000 visitors to Florida that season. The Florida Legislature issued an open invitation to wealthy investors with enactment of a constitutional amendment prohibiting income and inheritance taxes. The resulting capital influx accelerated an already well-developed surge of land purchases. Real estate sales mushroomed, quickly overinflating property values. Although the boom sprouted in south Florida, it flowered in virtually every city and town.

Most towns along the Indian River shared in the growth. Vero shed its agricultural character, exchanging fields and vacant lots for an urban setting with a commercial core, an industrial area, and distinctive residential neighborhoods. By contrast, Quay, Sebastian, Wabasso and other nearby villages retained their rural, agricultural trappings. Population growth encouraged residents of Sebastian, Vero, and Wabasso to incorporate their respective towns. The first of those was Vero, incorporated as the Town of Vero in 1919. Boosters adopted the slogans "Vigorous Vero" and "Watch Vero Grow," succeeded by "Vero, Where the Tropics Begin." Investors arrived from the Northeast and Midwest looking for land bargains. Over two hundred buildings rose between 1920 and 1927. In 1925, an expanding Town of Vero became the City of Vero Beach. During the boom, many municipal governments along the east coast appended the word "beach" to their legal names as a promotion gimmick.

The automobile changed the landscape and transformed society. Roads cuts through the countryside and bridges spanned the Indian River. The automobile gave access to a new class of Florida tourist. Once a winter resort for the wealthy, Florida became a haven for middle class families, who arrived in the summertime packed in automobiles. Many who came only to visit remained; others built seasonal residences.

Rising traffic along the east coast compelled the FEC to double track its mainline between Jacksonville and Miami and widen its bridges locally. The company nevertheless made few improvements to buildings between Sebastian and Oslo. In Vero Beach, city officials purchased the land for a new station and the Chamber of Commerce urged the FEC to build a new passenger station. Citing a statistic that five hundred winter residents had moved through the two-decades-old station in 1924, the chamber anticipated two thousand the following winter season. Members expressed concern that winter guests might abandon Vero Beach for cities with new stations. In 1926, the Chamber of Commerce drew plans for a new station, enlargement of the freight yard, and a bridge at the Twenty-fourth Street rail crossing. The plans were laid aside when the economy collapsed.

The two-story buff brick Wabasso School at 8895 U.S. Highway 1 was completed in 1925 at a cost of $30,000.

The Quay School was completed in 1919. A rising student population resulted in new classrooms in 1927, which complemented its Mission-styling.

Near the height of the boom, the FEC shuttled eighteen passenger trains daily between Jacksonville and Miami. The line adopted picturesque names such as "Dixie Flyer," "Key West Express," and "Everglades Limited" for its fast trains. S.M. Earling, son of the president of the Chicago, Milwaukee & St. Paul Railway, proposed a million-dollar Vero Beach and West Coast Railroad, a paper corporation that never moved off the drawing boards, but created a brief period of excitement in Vero Beach, promising residents of Indian River County a direct rail connection to Tampa. The powerful Seaboard Air Line Railroad (SAL) made inroads farther south along Florida's Atlantic coast. Operating 4,000

The lower photograph depicts the Vero school, built in 1919; the upper one a group of students posing at the front door of the building in the 1920s. Identified students in the group include Irene Sheffield, Alice Palmer, and Eunice Dean in the front row; and Dorothy Hennig, Florence Leffler. Hugh Poole and Paul Robertson in the back now.

Taken sometime after the close of the Great Florida Boom of the 1920s, this photograph shows downtown Vero Beach along Fourteenth Avenue, looking toward Twentieth Street (State Road 60).

miles of track in the Southeast, the SAL opened its Florida Western & Northern division in 1926, with rails extending from its mainline at Coleman in central Florida, through Sebring, across the north shore of Lake Okeechobee, to West Palm Beach and then to Hialeah. Although the SAL by-passed Indian River County, its appearance signaled significant growth in the region.

Improvements to the school system came with the good times. New brick buildings replaced inadequate wood-frame structures at Sebastian, Quay, Wabasso, and Vero. Fellsmere had gained an impressive masonry school in 1916. Vero's turn came in 1919 when the Jacksonville architectural firm of Mark & Sheftall drafted plans for a distinctive new building. The Vero school represented the first building in the community known to have been professionally designed. Contractors Fuquay & Gheen of Daytona Beach assembled the new building, whose buff brick exterior faced Nineteenth Street. At its dedication in 1919, the *Vero Press* boasted that "the school building is of Spanish architectural type which blends so well with the beautiful semi-tropical scenery of Vero." The building was expanded several times before 1925.

Residents called for the replacement of the wood-frame Quay school, built in 1908. Local school trustees selected a new site in 1917 and sold $5,000 in bonds in October 1918. Vero contractor J. Hudson Baker sketched the plans for the school, which displayed Mission Revival influences and contained two classrooms and an auditorium. G.N. & C.A. Woodward of Vero completed the building in 1919. A 1927 addition, designed by W.H. Wollen, cost a then-sizeable $5,200. Wabasso residents approved a school bond referendum in 1924. The school board selected Hatcher & Funke of Fort Pierce to prepare the plans for a new building, completed by the Cahow Construction Company in 1925.

In July 1925, following the creation of Indian River County, the school boards of Indian River and St. Lucie counties met to apportion the resources and debts the new county would assume. Indian River County assumed 43 percent of the existing debt and valuation. Residents elected W.E. Riggs as the superintendent of the newly-organized Indian River County School Board and Louis Harris, David

Rose, and R.W. Jamison as board members.

The new board assumed responsibility for constructing a Vero Beach High School. Hatcher & Funke of Fort Pierce, acknowledged for their work on previous projects, designed the school in the Italian Renaissance style to complement the graceful lines displayed by the adjacent Vero School. The Orlando-based J.C. Hanner Company was awarded the construction contract, which amounted to nearly $134,000. Development of Sebastian School, the last of the large boom-time projects in Indian River County, began in 1927. The board again turned to Hatcher & Funke for plans and approved W.H. Wollen's $43,000 construction bid. Controversy over both the design and site delayed completion until 1928, a year that brought financial trouble with the failure of the Farmer's Bank & Trust of Vero Beach, which held $36,781 of the School Board's deposits.

By the close of the decade, the school board maintained nine schools, four wood frame, and five masonry buildings. The last of the palmetto-log and one-room schoolhouses disappeared. Gifford and Wabasso also built schools for African-American pupils. The board enlisted the financial assistance of the Rosenwald Foundation to develop the Wabasso School. Organized by Chicago merchant and philanthropist Julius Rosenwald, by 1927, the foundation had provided $18 million in assistance for the construction of 4,000 rural schools in African-American communities. That year alone, the Rosenwald Foundation constructed over 400 schools. Rosenwald hired architects to develop a series of plans to fit various climates and school sizes. Wabasso's African-American school was assembled in 1928 by Vero contractor F.G. Fletcher at a cost of $3,600. After the building burned the following year, its students attended classes at a local church. The school board furnished bus transportation to black students living in outlying regions to schools at either Fellsmere, Gifford, or Wabasso.

Ray Redstone

Florida's booming economy in the years immediately following World War I attracted throngs of new residents, many of them seeking work. Ray Redstone's parents arrived in 1925, settling in what was then the town of Vero. Looking back, more than a half century later, Ray Redstone recalled a place of dirt roads, no electricity, a cook stove heated by kerosene and, like all other people with memories of those days, the "terrible mosquitoes." He remembers kerosene-soaked rags hanging in house windows, which provided some relief from the pests. His grandfather served on the Indian River County Board of County Commissioners and his uncle, B.T. Redstone, as mayor of Vero. During World War II, he said, many farmers raised castor beans, a source of castor oil, used for lubricating parts of aircraft.

The Vero Bridge, a wooden structure measuring thirty-two hundred feet in length, displayed a distinctive sweeping curve and a steel-truss center-pivot draw. Nearly 2,000 people attended the dedication in September 1920. The bridge reinvigorated development on the peninsula, which had remained essentially undeveloped since the arrival of the railroad a quarter-century earlier.

Growing use of the automobile required good roads and bridges. Indian River County's road construction programs formed part of a statewide system that promoted access to remote parts of the state. In 1918, only two bridges spanned the Indian River, those at Cocoa and Hobe Sound; farther north, seven bridges crossed the Halifax River between Ormond and New Smyrna. The Indian River structures were built and operated by county governments. Vero built the first span connecting the mainland and peninsula in St. Lucie County after approving a bridge district with taxing authority; which in 1919 sold $35,000 in bonds to finance the structure. A wooden structure 3,200 feet in length, the bridge displayed a distinctive sweeping curve with a steel center-pivot draw measuring 145 feet. Nearly 2,000 people attended the dedication in September 1920, looking on as 300 automobiles crossed the span. Building on the peninsula soon followed.

The completion of the bridge encouraged local government and peninsula dwellers to organize good roads from a patchwork of private trails and roads then providing limited transportation. In 1920, St. Lucie County designated a dirt trail on the peninsula a public road. Nearly fourteen miles long, the trail meandered past a schoolhouse and residences and made its way through citrus groves. Grubbed for stumps and roots during the 1920s and 1930s, the road, essentially a

dirt trail with a grass median, ran from the Vero bridge northward to the Brevard County line. It remained unpaved, though
nearby shell mounds were harvested for portions of its base.
Planted trees and shrubs that contributed to its ambiance and
provided scenic overlooks of the Indian River prompted the
Chamber of Commerce and businesses to advertise the road
on picture postcards. Later called the Jungle Trail, the road
was variously known as S.R. 252, A1A, the Inlet Road,
Narrows Road, Orchid Road, River Road, and the Vero Road.

*This photograph of
Indian River County's
Jungle Trail north of
Old Winter Beach Road
show the trail as it
appeared about 1935.*

Development
pressures and public outcries
over the proposals to abandon
the road in 1983 and 1986
resulted in the designation of
Jungle Trail north of the Old
Winter Beach Bridge Road as an
official Florida Greenway and a
historic landscape.

The Riomar community, an
early exclusive peninsular development, benefitted from the
completion of the Vero bridge
and peninsular road construction.
Riomar was founded in 1919 as
the East View Development
Company by Cleveland, Ohio
residents W.H. Humiston, John P.
Sawyer, and E.E. Strong. The so-
called "Cleveland colonists"
bought the tract from Herman

Dr. W. H. Humiston

Zeuch for $8,500. Seasonal visitors, the Riomar founders initially laid out a subdi-
vision with fifty-two lots that stretched from river-to-ocean and a few years later
doubled its size. In total, the subdivision offered ninety-six building lots, a yacht
club, a forty-acre country club, and a nine-hole golf course designed by E.E.
Smith. Alex MacWilliam of Cleveland, the first club manager, later served several
terms as mayor of Vero Beach and one term in the Florida Legislature.

Arthur G. McKee House, 1922.

The founders of Riomar were influential scholars and physicians from Cleveland, Ohio. One of the first people to build at Riomar, John P. Sawyer served as professor of clinical medicine and therapeutics at Case Western Reserve University. W.H. Humiston, a professor of medicine at Case Western Reserve, served as president of the Cleveland Medical Society and later as president of Vero Beach's Beautification Society. Humiston's "Canary Cottage" was one of the first houses built at Riomar. Within a few years, Winchester Fitch of Connecticut built a $50,000 estate at Riomar. Renowned engineer Arthur G. McKee also built a fashionable seasonal dwelling, directing H.G. Dill, the manager of his Cleveland engineering company, to supervise construction. Completed in 1922, the house featured a distinctive Mediterranean Revival flair with stucco and oyster shell exterior wall finishes. Other early Riomar homeowners and seasonal visitors included the Baker, Coit and Comstock families, and John C. Hale, a circuit judge from Cleveland, Ohio. Most residents during the 1920s owned houseboats or yachts and several belonged to the exclusive Manusing Beach Club at Rye, New York, the design of which was applied to the Riomar Bay Yacht Club.

Riomar residents welcome President Warren G. Harding to their winter colony in January 1921.

Riomar's residents formed the core of Vero Beach's "Ohio winter colony." In January 1921, following news of a twelve-day cruise on the Indian River by president-elect Warren G. Harding, a native of Marion, Ohio, Riomar residents prevailed upon the new chief executive to anchor his houseboat, *Victoria,* at their dock and play a round of golf there. Harding's visit briefly put Vero on the front pages of the nation's newspapers, including the *New York Times.* Harding later sailed to Miami, and on his return voyage anchored overnight near Sebastian. On a second visit to Vero in March 1923 as part of an eighteen-day, six hundred mile cruise aboard the houseboat *Pioneer,* the president played another round of golf at Riomar. Following Harding's sudden death in August 1923, residents of Highlands and Okeechobee counties gave his name to a bridge that crossed the Kissimmee River on State Road 70.

The construction of the Vero bridge and initial success of Riomar prompted additional local developments. The Beachland Development Company began in 1922 to organize Vero Beach Estates, the first large subdivision on the peninsula, though land sales did not commence until early 1925. Spreading along the ocean front north of Riomar, Vero Beach Estates was divided by Beachland Boulevard, which was connected to the Vero bridge. The subdivision contained 20 blocks and nearly 1,000 building lots. The principal investor, Atlanta realtor C.C. Braswell, also built the Beachland Casino, which included a swimming pool filled by pumped-in ocean water. Braswell eventually sold his shares in the Beachland Development Company to James O. Watson of West Palm Beach, who built one of the first elaborate dwellings at Vero Beach Estates. The company sold several hundred building lots before the end of the decade.

Constructed about 1915, the Twitchell Building stood on the south side of Twentieth Street between Fourteenth and Fifteenth Avenues. Typical of early twentieth century dual-use buildings, it contained a general store on the first floor and residential space on the second. The building burned to the ground in a November 1919 fire that swept away the entire block. The conflagration changed the face of the town and altered attitudes about the use of building materials. Virtually all downtown buildings were constructed with brick or ceramic hollow tiles following the fire.

The Vero Beach Villas subdivision, opened in March 1926, stretched from the ocean to the river south of Riomar. It contained 77 blocks and nearly 2,000 building sites. Finger islands protruded into the river for exclusive residential sites. To facilitate travel between the mainland and its subdivision, the company financed the construction of a quarter million dollar bridge, completed with a sixty-foot steel bascule in 1927. Veromar, the last of the large boom-time subdivisions on the peninsula, was organized by investors from Palm Beach County in May 1925. It occupied two hundred sixty acres between the river and ocean near Bethel Creek and Vero Beach Estates. Curved streets and parks decorated the fifty-two block neighborhood, which contained nearly 1,300 building sites. The subdivision's northeast corner was defined by a large park immediately south of the Bethel Creek House of Refuge. Most of its lots remained unsold when the land boom collapsed.

On November 16, 1919, a fire consumed four of Vero's downtown buildings. The conflagration altered the face of the town and changed opinions about the use of building materials. About three o'clock on that fateful November morning, Mrs. C.E. Sandison discovered a blaze in the Twitchell Building and a nearby boarding house. The flames soon spread to adjacent wood-frame structures and within hours consumed the entire south side of Osceola Boulevard between

Pocahantas Building

In the century's first decade, Vero's Sleepy Eye Lodge and the Seminole Building began a tradition of naming buildings after Native Americans. The Pocahontas Arcade, built in 1923 at the corner of Fourteenth Avenue and Twenty-first Street, initially contained nine offices. Complete with a wrap-around loggia, its commercial success led to a second-story addition in 1926. On the parapet, artist A.A. Thomas sculpted a life-size image of the Indian maiden Pocahontas.

Seminole and Cherokee Avenues. A light rain prevented sparks from setting fire to still more houses and buildings. Residents attributed the blaze to a cigarette carelessly thrown into a pool room corner. In all, Maher's Department Store, Trice's Boarding House, Twitchell's Pool Room and Barber Shop, Allison Brothers Grocery and the Victory Restaurant were reduced to ashes. In the wake of the blaze, an ordinance specified the use of brick or masonry for building construction in the commercial area. New masonry commercial buildings soon occupied the site of the destruction.

A second, more dramatic fire in October 1921 that swept away $31,000 worth of buildings spurred the creation of a fire department. The blaze began east of the FEC tracks in Lee Howard's wood-frame cottage. Heat and sparks ignited the nearby warehouse of the Redstone Lumber Company, creating great alarm because the building contained dynamite. Explosions soon rocked the earth, propelling burning embers to the nearby Indian River Farms Company packing house. The two buildings created a sensational fire that burned for hours, consuming adjacent telephone poles. B.T. and C.G. Redstone rebuilt their business and went on to supply many of the building materials that changed the architectural landscape of downtown Vero during the boom years.

A number of skilled carpenters and builders contributed to the architectural fabric of Vero and Indian River County. Among the earliest and most prolific was J. Hudson Baker, who arrived in Vero about 1915 from Kansas City. His home was the first dwelling constructed on lands reclaimed by the Indian River Farms Company. With Rollen Martin, Baker formed the Vero Building Company in 1919 and constructed countless houses over the following decades. Baker assembled Vero's Sleepy Eye Lodge, Farmers Bank, First Methodist Church, Mattmueller and O'Malley buildings, additions to Vero Elementary School and R.R. Riccou's brick store in Fort Pierce. Blackford and Davis built the Pocahontas and Pueblo arcades. Other builders who arrived in Vero by 1920 included Even & Brunen;

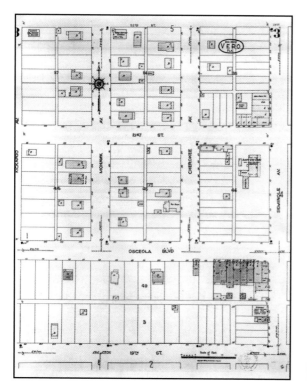

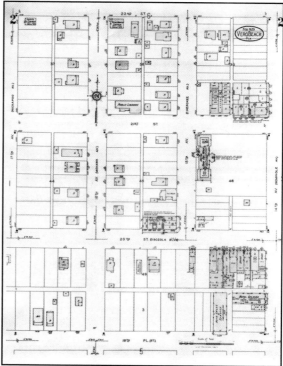

Harrison, Mayfield & Bohner; Lawrence M. Newman; G.N. & C.A Woodward; and Vero Concrete Company.

Speculation and investment income fueled Vero's development. In 1925 contractor Fred King built eight bungalows for rental income in Osceola Park subdivision. T.E. Harrison, a Nebraska builder who had constructed the home of renowned orator and politician William Jennings Bryan in Lincoln, arrived in Vero in 1924 and at once announced the construction of twenty-five speculative homes. By then, Harrison had built dwellings for Walter Buckingham and Laurence Dorsey in the town's fashionable Royal Park subdivision. Elaborately executed in 1925, the $80,000 Farmers Bank displayed fanciful Byzantine and Mediterranean Revival influences. These projects spurred still more construction by other investors. The Campbell Arcade, Pueblo Arcade, and Royal Park Arcade followed in 1926.

Notable among the city's architects was William H. Garns of Indianapolis. Garns first visited Vero Beach in 1925 at the height of the land boom. He set up a local office and won commissions to design the Campbell Arcade, the Gleckler Apartment Building, and several residences. In 1927, following the collapse of the land boom, Garns returned to his home state, but returned later to design the

Prepared by the Sanborn Map Company of New York, these maps illustrate the expansion of several blocks of Vero Beach between 1923 and 1929. Although relatively few residential buildings were constructed in the area during the interval, commercial activity surged forward.

In 1925, the Vero Beach Press boasted "No city has better protection from fire than has Vero Beach with these men always on the job." Dramatic fires in 1919 compelled Vero's newly-formed municipal government to invest in reliable fire fighting equipment. In this scene, the city's volunteer fire-fighting staff pose on their new trucks, decked out in their hats and slickers. Behind them stands the city hall, which had been built in 1922. The city hall then occupied a site at the northeast corner of Thirteenth Avenue and Twentieth Street. Hailed as one of the "grandest buildings in Vero," the city hall contained the fire department, jail, meeting hall, and municipal offices.

Indian River County Courthouse and several fashionable residences. Chicago architect William Krieg, who launched his career in 1893, planned the expansive Indrio development in St. Lucie County and won commissions to design the Hotel Vero Del Mar and the Beachland Casino. A splendid example of Mediterranean Revival architecture, the Del Mar occupied a prominent site at the corner of Fourteenth Avenue and Twenty-first Street. Upon opening in August 1927, the Beachland Casino, located on the beach at the end of S. R. 60, was boasted to be the "largest and most complete structure of its kind on the East Coast between Daytona Beach and Palm Beach."

William Hatcher and Lawrence Funke, based in Fort Pierce, specialized in school design. Their commissions in St. Lucie County include Fort Pierce's First United Methodist Church, the Fort Pierce City Hall, the Okeechobee High School, and the White City School; and in Indian River County the Wabasso School, Vero Beach High School, and the Sebastian School. The firm also designed several projects for the Vero Beach Construction Company, including the Ocean Front Apartments, three apartment buildings on Nineteenth Avenue and the Royal Park Arcade.

Downtown construction in Vero spread to the city's outskirts. Edgewood Addition and Osceola Park, which opened in 1916 and 1917, continued to offer attractive building sites south of the growing commercial center. The Hoosier Realty Company, organized in 1916 by seasonal visitors from Terre Haute, Indiana, advertised its Edgewood Addition in the Midwest. The company enjoyed a brief period of success. A small "Indiana colony" of seasonal visitors, such as the Gammons and Mills families, built cottages. Growth in those subdivisions accelerated in the 1920s. The Palmetto Hotel, listed in the National Register, was constructed in 1921 by George W. Gray on Dixie Highway. Farther west, H.C. Sherwood of Bridgeport, Connecticut and dentist John Leroy Hutchison, who served as sales manager of the Indian River Farms Company, developed estates in 1919. In March 1920, the Vero Building Company reported it had recently constructed and sold eight bungalows. Home buyers included A.A Potter of Kansas City; Mrs. H.B. Talley of Winchester, Tennessee; Charles Kirk of

Paintsville, Kentucky; and Mrs. Charles Mount of Hightown, New Jersey. The *Vero Press* eagerly ran chatterbox columns reporting construction activity and proposed developments.

Property prices and sales skyrocketed. In September 1925, near the height of the land boom, the city government in Vero issued over $300,000 in building permits. Over sixty residential subdivisions were platted and scores of individual residences planned. A few subdivisions featured elaborate designs along with restrictions on costs of construction and design. In contrast to the conventional grid system, the Royal Park and McAnsh Park subdivisions featured curved streets and irregular building lots.

To add appeal to its subdivision, the Royal Park Company included a golf course in its development. Waldo Sexton, Warren Zeuch, and several other golfers pose on a fairway about 1927. In the 1930s, the nine-hole course was expanded to eighteen holes.

Royal Park became Indian River County's fashionable mainland subdivision. The Royal Park Company, organized in August 1923 by Waldo Sexton, Walter S. Buckingham, F.L. Hemmings, and Arthur G. McKee, fashioned 1,000 acres of residential lots out of a jungle-like tract between the railroad tracks and the shore of the Indian River north of Twentieth Street. W.G. Eager, a graduate of the University of Pennsylvania who practiced architecture in Valdosta, Georgia, laid out the design for a nine-hole golf course. Fort Pierce architect John Sherwood designed the club house. The original names of streets conjured images of the

These picturesque houses decorated the Royal Park subdivision in the 1920s. Many of the thirty residences and seven apartment buildings belonged to seasonal residents, such as John A. Meyer, a Milwaukee businessman. The Meyer house, pictured at the left, was photographed and printed on a picture postcard, which was distributed by the company to help persuade potential buyers to invest in Vero Beach property. The house shown to the right illustrates the Mediterranean style, popular in that decade.

This building is representative of the large investments made by seasonal visitors in Indian River County real estate during the 1920s. In June 1926, Clayton Gleckler hired Vero Beach architect William Garns to draft the plans for the apartment building. Completed later that year in the fashionable Mediterranean Revival genre, the building included a "luxurious lounging room" on the third floor.

2 KILLED, 1 WOUNDED AS POSSES BATTLE EVERGLADE BANDITS

Sheriff, Leader of Ashley-Mobley Gang and Woman Are Victims in All-Day Fight.

STRONGHOLD IS ATTACKED

Officers Drive Robbers From Lair With a Machine Gun and Fierce Running Fight Follows.

7 TAKEN, OTHERS ESCAPE

Gang Had Terrorized Florida Ten Years and Lately Turned to Hijacking and Piracy.

WEST PALM BEACH, Fla., Jan. 9 (Associated Press).—Two men were killed and a woman was injured today during a day-long fight between officers and citizens with the Ashley-Mobley band of outlaws in the Florida Everglades, twenty-six miles north of here. The officers, using machine guns, fired on the outlaws' camp early this morning.

The exploits of the Ashley-Mobley gang attracted national attention, as this headline in the January 10, 1924 edition of the New York Times reveals

state's Spanish heritage, such as Catalina, Coronado, Laurel, Paloma, Pine, Ponce de Leon, and Royal Palm. Hotelier Frederick Doeschner of Pittsburg opened the Royal Park Inn, the gem of the development, in November 1924.

Seasonal resident John A. Meyer, a Milwaukee businessman, built one of the first dwellings in Royal Park. His home, located on Royal Palm Boulevard, was pictured on a penny postcard, which the company distributed to advertise its development. In May 1926, the company claimed that 30 dwellings and 7 apartment buildings, valued at $435,000, had been constructed in Royal Park. E.A. Byrkit and Thomas Ward built two-story residences on Fairway Drive. Florence Harrison and Phillip Shaner built houses on Laurel Drive. Walter James' house overlooked the links on Valencia Drive. Builder Lawrence M. Newman constructed a one-story apartment building with a central courtyard on Granada Avenue. Architect William Garns designed a large apartment building on Royal Palm Boulevard for Clayton B. Gleckler of Punxutawney, Pennsylvania, complete with a "luxurious lounging room" on the third floor. E.P. Waldron of Pontiac, Michigan engaged Orlando architect Frederick Trimble to design a seasonal residence overlooking the golf course. By mid-1926, the developers estimated that over $1 million had been spent at Royal Park in land clearing, road and house construction, installation of plants and ornamentals, and golf course construction.

In an era when crime figures often dominated newspaper reports, the Indian River region found its own stars in the so-called Ashley-Mobley Gang. John Ashley began his life of crime in Miami before moving to Gomez, a small village south of Stuart. There, with his sons Joe, John, Bob, and Bill, Ashley farmed and hunted in the Everglades, before turning to bootlegging and banditry. Joined by relatives and

Harvesting citrus provided hundreds of jobs in Indian River County during the 1920s. Planned and financed by O. O. Helseth, Charles H. McKee, and Waldo Sexton, the Oslo Packing House was completed in October 1920. Vero contractor L. M. Newman assembled the building, one of the first large packing houses constructed in the county. Albert O. Helseth served as the first manager of the house.

friends, including Hanford Mobley, Wesley Mobley, Ray Lynn, and Bob Middleton, the bandits became known as the Ashley-Mobley Gang. A murder in 1911 and bank robberies in Stuart and Miami in 1915 escalated into wholesale plunder of the southeast coast, which included holding up banks and railroad stations. The gang even turned to piracy on the high seas, preying on liquor distributors in the Bahamas and smugglers plying the waters between the Bahamas and Miami. Gang members became fugitives of federal, state, and local authorities, and the British government.

The *New York Times* characterized the gang as brought up in "the Jesse James school of felony...in the true western-story manner." Newspapers credited their ability to elude capture for over a decade to a well-concealed hideout near Fruita and close knowledge of the Everglades. Although two members drowned at sea, most of the Ashley-Mobley gangsters died violent deaths in shoot outs with law enforcement officials. In 1924, after a robbery at the Stuart Bank and Trust, Sheriff J.R. Merritt of St. Lucie County led a posse to the gang's hideout. In a day-long battle, the posse killed several gangsters and captured seven others. The surviving fugitives, including John Ashley, Shorty Lynn, Robert Middleton, and Hanford Mobley, met their end in early in November 1924 on the Sebastian River Bridge at Stuart, where they were trapped and shot dead by law officers. On several occasions, The *New York Times* gave the gang and its exploits front-page coverage.

But for swarms of mosquitoes, most Indian River residents lived relatively comfortable lives. Vero citrus topped the national markets in March 1920, when wholesalers paid more per box for locally-grown fruit than the best oranges offered by California planters. The Vero Top brand, packed by the Vero Fruit Growers Association, sold for $8.88 per box and Deerfield Groves' Golden brand, the third highest priced orange on the New York market that season, brought $7.28 per box. Most California oranges then sold for $7.11 per box, while the average Florida orange netted $6 per box. Vero's Charles Gifford, manager of the Growers Association, proudly advertised Vero Top as "one of the world's five leading brands." The "orange gold" fever accelerated in 1922, when over four hundred rail cars arrived in New York filled with fruit shipped by Oslo, Vero, and Wabasso packers. Vero's AFG packing house again took top honors, selling its "Brights" in New York for $9.50 per box. Indian River fruit, by then already well-known to those familiar with the fruit market, secured its enduring national reputation in the early 1920s.

Commercially successful, Vero Beach chafed under the political supervision of county officials in Fort Pierce, twenty miles to the south. Just as Fort Pierce residents had agitated for county division two decades before, Vero Beach community leaders began pushing for a county seat of their own. It was a familiar story in fast-growing Florida, where thirteen new counties were formed between 1921 and 1925. As early as 1919, controversy arose between residents

Facing west, this scene captures the Vero Theater and the Farmer's Bank under construction. The Vero Theater opened October 1924 with the feature film "Hunchback of Notre Dame." Within six months of its opening, the theater became the center of a county division fight that ended with the creation of Indian River County in May 1925.

of Fort Pierce and Vero, when a faction of Vero residents, known as "dyed-in-the-wool and blown-in-the-bottle good-roads boosters," lost a bond referendum for county-wide road improvements. Blaming Fort Pierce voters for the defeat, local attorney and *Vero Press* editor Paul Nisle caustically observed: "Good roads aren't needed in St. Lucie County. They are not necessary to drive cattle over . . . ." A year later the two cities did reach a compromise on a smaller package of road bonds, but the seeds of division had been planted.

Blue laws, a residue of Victorian Era morality, provoked even greater and more lasting conflict. St. Lucie County Sheriff Ruffner set off the controversy in 1922 by shutting down all business transactions on Sundays. Vero merchants obeyed the order and "not a cigar nor a cold drink nor a gallon of gas was sold." Fort Pierce businessmen, however, largely ignored the law. Sheriff deputies roamed the city's streets, recording the names of offenders. Vero residents prided themselves on obeying the law, but two years later a new and more bitter legal issue emerged to divide the two communities.

Vero's first theater, the Strand, opened in 1917 in a wooden building. William Atkin and Freeman Knight purchased the business about 1920 amid a booming economy. Three years later they organized the Vero Theater Corporation and hired Orlando architect Frederick Trimble to draft plans for a new theater. The completed theater opened in October 1924 with a showing of the "Hunchback of Notre Dame." Over six hundred seats filled the auditorium and a $10,000 Fotoplayer organ provided accompaniment to the silent film. The building itself, cast in the popular Mediterranean style of the era, was an architectural gem.

But the theater's management insisted on showing movies on Sundays. On February 15, 1925, frustrated by repeated snubbing of a law prohibiting business

---

Sarah B. Cockrell-Atkin

William Atkin, the father of Sarah Cockrell-Atkin, leased a railroad car for $267 and moved his family and belongings from New Jersey to Vero in 1914. But Atkin and his family encountered a problem upon arrival: the house they were moving into contained only four rooms and "we had eight rooms of furniture," Sarah Cockrell-Atkin recalled. Her father came to Florida because "Judge Andrews wanted Papa to open a bank." What became the Vero Bank and Trust Atkin initially started in a small frame building with one safe. He later built the Florida Theater, which opened October 20, 1924 with a showing of "The Hunchback of Notre Dame." A newspaper clipping from the time, which Sarah Cockrell-Atkin displayed when she was interviewed by the Indian River County Historical Society in 1988, reported that the organ for the theater was purchased in California and shipped to Florida through the Panama Canal. Until about 1930, movies had no sound. An organist in the theater played a musical accompaniment to the silent events that unfolded on the screen.

on Sunday, sheriff's officers from Fort Pierce "stopped the show," in the words of the *Vero Press,* turning on the house lights and ordering patrons to leave the building. They then arrested manager William Atkin, operator Henry Metz, and ticket seller William Frick. Angered to the core, William Atkin, who was also president of the Vero Bank and Trust Company, obtained an injunction from circuit court Judge C.E. Chillingworth of West Palm Beach ordering the sheriff to refrain from interfering with future Sunday showings. The sheriff ignored the court order and the following Sunday served arrest warrants on the theater owner and his workers. The dispute drew regional attention and the legal community chose sides.

Disgruntled by what they perceived as the sheriff's unnecessary meddling in local affairs, Vero businessmen and the local chamber of commerce persuaded State Representative A. W. Young to introduce a bill into the state legislature creating Indian River County, carving the new jurisdiction out of St. Lucie County. Young, elected to the state legislature in1921, had a share of ownership in the theater company. He was also mayor of Vero. Efforts by Fort Pierce leaders to kill Young's initiative were derailed when citizens in Stuart, south of Fort Pierce, launched a similar drive to create still another county out of the southern part of St. Lucie County and the northern part of Palm Beach County. Young

This May 1925 scene depicts a contingent of Vero Beach "county divisionists" at the train shed at Tallahassee's railroad station. Behind them stands the "Indian River County Special," a specially-chartered train that carried the activists between Vero Beach and Tallahassee. At the state capital, they successfully lobbied the Florida Legislature to create Indian River County. They returned home victorious and persuaded voters in the new county to select Vero as the county seat of government.

A. W. YOUNG

gained Governor John W. Martin's support for the divisions by suggesting that the proposed southern county be named after the governor. In early May 1925, nearly seventy area businessmen and residents took an "Indian River County Special" train to Tallahassee to press for legislative approval.

Young, who served as chair of the house committee on county organization, steered the measure through his committee to a floor vote and then into the Florida Senate, where it passed after vigorous debate. The Fort Pierce forces capitulated when the bill's Vero supporters agreed to move the south boundary of the proposed county three miles northward to a line that separated the Indian River Farms Drainage District from the Fort Pierce Farms Drainage District. On May 25, 1925, Governor Martin signed the bill creating Indian River County, Florida's sixty-fifth county jurisdiction. Young's successful strategy won him the undying loyalty of local residents. Georgia native and Vero Beach attorney James T. Vocelle observed that the episode pitted "what might be referred to as a 'cracker town'" against the "Yankees" of Vero Beach. Vero Beach residents rejoiced when residents of the new county selected their city as the seat of government. Offices of the new county government were installed in the Seminole Building on Seminole Avenue. Three-time presidential candidate William Jennings Bryan, famed for his oratorical skills, delivered the principal speech at a victory celebration in Vero Beach.

The neighboring community of Quay, formed in 1902, shared in the euphoria. Subdivision of that area began in 1921, when C.H. Fletcher created Fletcher's Addition. In 1924, Donald Forbes and J.J. Hamilton opened Quay Subdivision. Atlanta developer C.C. Braswell, who had purchased all of the undeveloped lots in both Fletcher's Addition and Forbes and Hamilton's subdivision, challenged residents to dump the designation Quay for a more appealing name. His selection committee settled on "Winter Beach," a name submitted by Mrs. Robert Brown of Fort Pierce, who earned a lot valued at $1,000 for her winning entry. Braswell

---

The Cadenhead Family

The Cadenhead family of five spent a week in 1922 traveling on trains, ferries, and in an old Buick, moving from Alabama to Vero. The real estate boom that began in the wake of World War I attracted T.R. Cadenhead, Sr. to Florida. In business with C.B. Osteen, he opened a store and filling station. His wife ran the Cozy Cafe, where, T.R. Cadenhead, Jr. recalled in a 1988 interview, "you could get a fish dinner for 75 cents." Initially, neither electricity or running water was available. The family used oil lamps to read by and pumped water from a cistern. When he was not in school, young T.R. spent his time fishing, playing marbles, and hunting. "I always had a sling shot in my back pocket, and I never considered wearing shoes until Vero High," he recalled.

composed catchy slogans, such as "Winter Beach, Where Sunshine Spends the Winter," for the newly-named town. Braswell boasted that his development contained 800 acres and 8,000 building lots. Despite his extensive sales efforts, Winter Beach failed to meet Braswell's expectations.

Wabasso likewise enjoyed only moderate growth. Thirty-six registered voters met in the Deerfield Groves Company hotel in August 1925 to form a municipal government. They elected J.L. Powers as mayor, W.F. Cox as clerk, and T.R. Cadenhead, Joseph Ebby, W.T. Jones, George Sears, and Clarence Vandiver as aldermen. Paul Hood served as town marshall. New developments sprinkled the landscape. John Menge of Virginia opened a twenty-seven acre subdivision he named Weona Park, which contained ten blocks divided by Hibiscus, Palm, and Poinsettia boulevards east of the Dixie Highway. T.R. Cadenhead, L.B. O'Steen, and Mary Whittington incorporated the Wabasso Mercantile Company in 1927. In the Eureka Estates subdivision, C. Frank Reed installed thirty-five electric standards, creating one of the first so-called "whiteways" in the county. Joseph Ebby of Cleveland, Ohio constructed a Mediterranean Revival-style dwelling on Greenwood Street.

Wabasso citrus growers shipped 340 rail cars of fruit in 1925, far surpassing other parts of the county. Built in the early 1920s, the AFG's main east coast packing house stood at Wabasso. Early Wabasso settler George Sears reported a record profit of $5,200 from his 4-acre grove, most of it planted in grapefruit. The Sebastian Land Company shipped seventy-seven rail cars of tomatoes and four cars of watermelons. The company also maintained a turpentine camp in a 30,000-acre tract west of town. Completion in 1928 of the Wabasso Bridge, a $75,000 project built by the Austin Brothers Bridge Company of Atlanta, Georgia, promised easier movement of crops from the peninsula to packing houses in Wabasso. The bridge measured 5,800 feet with a steel center-pivot draw fabricated by the N.T. Harlow Company of Jacksonville.

Sebastian residents approved municipal incorporation in 1924. The new town council, which included Mayor T.B. Hicks and aldermen C.L. Beugnot, M.M. Miller, A.G. Roberts, H.M. Sallee, and Charles Sembler, reincorporated as a city in 1925. When the Dixie Highway arrived in 1924, the city installed gateway arches across the roadway. The Vickers Brothers, owners of a 1913 subdivision in Sebastian, constructed the town's first modern hollow-tile commercial block in 1925. The Sebastian Woman's Club, organized in 1914, completed a clubhouse in 1928, the same year the new masonry school was dedicated.

The land boom of the 1920s touched most areas of Florida. About 1926, the San Sebastian Development Company published a promotional booklet highlighting the advantages of living in Indian River County. These three photographs depict the entrance into the development. Known as the "Sun Porch of America," the San Sebastian development maintained its headquarters on Fifth Avenue in New York and Bradley Place in Palm Beach; motorist driving along a nearby stretch of recently-paved U.S. Highway 1; and the reinforced-concrete St. Sebastian River Bridge. Like other developments, it became bankrupt after the collapse of the land boom.

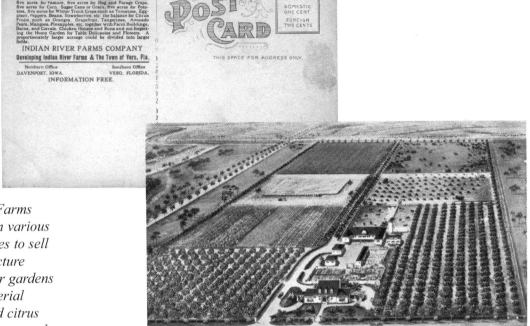

This sub-division of a forty-acre farm and home arrangement comprising attractiveness and horticultural beautification with a variety of crops for profit. Dividing the tract thru the center with a roadway from either side of which are fields: five acres for Pasture, five acres for Hog and Forage Crops, five acres for Corn, Sugar Cane or Grain, five acres for Potatoes, five acres for Winter Truck Crops such as Tomatoes, Egg-plant, Peppers, Beans, Strawberries, etc: the balance for Citrus Fruits, such as Oranges, Grapefruit, Tangerines, Avocado Pears, Mangoes, Pineapples, etc. together with Farm Buildings, Barns, and Corrals, Chicken Houses and Runs and not forgetting the Home Garden for Table Delicacies and Flowers. A proportionately larger acreage could be divided into larger fields.

INDIAN RIVER FARMS COMPANY
Developing Indian River Farms & The Town of Vero, Fla.

Northern Office   Southern Office
DAVENPORT, IOWA.   VERO, FLORIDA.
INFORMATION FREE.

POST CARD

PLACE STAMP HERE
DOMESTIC ONE CENT
FOREIGN TWO CENTS

THIS SPACE FOR ADDRESS ONLY.

AN IDEAL SUBDIVISION FOR A FORTY-ACRE TRACT IN INDIAN RIVER FARMS AT VERO, FLORIDA.

The Indian River Farms Company relied on various promotional devices to sell land, including picture postcards of flower gardens and picturesque aerial views of farms and citrus groves. The company used catchy slogans, such as "The Rich Man's Playground is fast becoming the Poor Man's Paradise," to attract buyers. Aerial views often depicted large tracts with a home, farm buildings, chicken houses, gardens, and well-defined fields and groves planted in various crops, all embraced by large canals.

The major highways and railroads that brought thousands of visitors and speculators to the state's urban centers and to villages along the Indian River skirted the remote agricultural community of Fellsmere. While most peninsular businesses enjoyed unprecedented growth, both the Bank of Fellsmere and the Fellsmere Supply Company failed. The Citizen's Bank, established in 1924, lasted only one year. A newly-organized Fellsmere Company sold its holdings to the Standard Agricultural Chemical Company in 1923, renamed the following year as the Ammoniate Products Corporation. Only some twenty-five building were constructed in Fellsmere. The congregation of Fellsmere Methodist Church, founded in 1914, completed a new sanctuary in 1924 on Broadway. Corydon Nourse, a native of Ohio who arrived in 1918 and a member of the church, prepared the plans and supervised construction. Nourse also built the Mission-style Fellsmere Estates Corporation Building on Broadway. Completed about 1926, the building housed the business offices of the Ammoniate Products Corporation. In the 1930s, the Estates Building contained the offices of the Fellsmere Sugar Company, which helped save the city from economic ruin. These two buildings represent the high point of activity in Fellsmere during the land boom.

The air began to seep out of Florida's speculative land bubble in late 1925. In August, the FEC announced an embargo on freight shipments to south Florida, where ports and rail terminals were clogged with unused building supplies. As land sales declined and construction slowed, it became clear that many highly-leveraged subdivisions faced financial ruin. Banks collapsed, reorganized, and failed again. Investors vanished. Amid it all, south Florida was struck in 1926 and 1928 by devastating hurricanes that leveled communities and killed thousands, providing a sad closing chapter to an era of wild speculation.

The Florida State Chamber of Commerce attempted to revive the state's shattered national image with advertising campaigns. As part of a "Picture Postcard Week," residents were asked to mail picturesque views of their communities to out-of-state friends. The Vero Beach Chamber of Commerce was assigned the first week of October 1928. Residents were encouraged to claim that the storm damage was not as widespread or severe as reported. Even school children were inveighed to send postcards, at least one each week. The chamber assumed responsibility for supplying the postage and mailing the cards.

Indeed, scenic vistas along the Indian River and depressed land prices attracted some wealthy investors. At Riomar, a small building boom began in 1928 with construction of a landmark house for Elliott Phillips, president of the DeVoe & Reynolds Paint Manufacturing Company of New York City. Phillips had married Katherine Fitch, the daughter of seasonal resident Winchester Fitch, who lived in Greenwich, Connecticut, and had built a large house near the river several years earlier. Although it appears hard to believe now, the Phillips mansion was, in 1929, the only residence between Daytona Beach and Palm Beach situated beside the ocean. Palm Beach contractor J.R. Wakeman supervised construction of the $50,000 house, which was designed by prominent Palm Beach architect Howard B. Major. Possessing an unrivaled view of the Atlantic Ocean and containing 3,900 square feet of interior floor space, the Phillips Mansion became part of the Indian River region's resort architecture and among the first of Major's commissions in Indian River County.

The Riomar "chateau" of Alexander S. Taylor, a prominent Cleveland, Ohio realtor, followed the Phillips mansion. Taylor's house, executed in 1929 in the Mediterranean Revival genre, contributed to the exclusivity of Riomar and the resort image of the peninsula. Taylor, a former president of the National

Association of Real Estate Boards, helped conceptualize and push through a plan adopted by Vero Beach officials for a local airport. A site was selected northwest of the McAnsh Park subdivision and a lease arrangement negotiated for the land with Cadillac dealer Bud Holman.

Despite the bleak economy, citrus production remained high. The Sebastian Land Company, with 30,000 acres near Wabasso, was reorganized as the Indian River Fruit Growers, Inc. and in 1929 began planting an additional 2,400 acres of orange trees. In Vero Beach, the McKee-Sexton Land Company embarked on an ambitious program to plant 1,000 acres in citrus. By decade's end, the Vero Beach region alone claimed one-hundred-five farms, Winter Beach ninety-eight, Gifford fifty-six, and Fellsmere forty-four. Investments in farmlands and buildings, implements, and machinery reached $6.5 million in 1930. By then, the faint outlines of an agribusiness economy within the county began to emerge.

Much had occurred in the region surrounding Vero Beach in the halcyon decade that followed World War I. The new county witnessed substantial agricultural expansion, emergence of a strong local economy based on the building trades, and a gathering of significant political clout. Large citrus-producing corporations provided money and influence. In the great crash that accompanied the end of the boom, many Indian River County residents suffered financial reverses and others actually experienced a financial windfall. Sagging property values and foreclosed properties attracted investors fortunate enough to have escaped financial ruin in the crash. During the depression decade that followed the Great Crash, Vero Beach and Indian River County provided an island of comparative relief from the surrounding sea of economic misery.

Chapter Six
Great Depression, New Deal, and World War II, 1929-1945

ALTHOUGH CONTINUING DEMAND FOR CITRUS PRODUCTS buoyed the local economy during the Great Depression, Indian River County did not escape unscathed. The Bank of Sebastian and Farmers Bank in Vero Beach counted themselves among the scores of Florida banks that failed as deposits and investments fell and personal income declined. Still, the county grew. The population rose from 6,700 in 1930 to nearly 9,000 ten years later, a rate of growth that placed it sixth in the state. In that same period, Vero Beach's population climbed from 2,268 to 3,060. Most towns in the county experienced similar expansion: Fellsmere from 356 to 643 residents; Wabasso from 300 to 998; and Sebastian from 386 to 425.

To accommodate the rising number of visitors and new residents, Indian River County enlisted in an ambitious state road construction program. In the waning years of the 1920s, the county completed a $650,000 road building project and through a legislative act that formed a multi-county road district, cooperated in constructing State Road 60, which ran to Tampa and was then known as the Ocean-to-Gulf Highway. So intense was the traffic upon the road that hardly a decade later it needed improvement. E.G. Thatcher of the Vero Beach Chamber of Commerce thought the improvements too slow, for the road was closed during the 1936-1937 tourist season. The road furnished an important link between Vero Beach and the federal highways that ran down the center of the peninsula. Thatcher pointed to the absence of tourists coming from the west and claimed that "The long delay in this matter has caused us heavy loss, and has been seriously protested, but to no avail." Once a winter resort for the wealthy, Florida had become a vacation mecca for families who traveled by automobile. The loss of that market, for even a single season, jeopardized the local economy.

Waterway improvement became an issue equal in significance to highway construction. Although only the wealthiest of tourists arrived by yacht, these

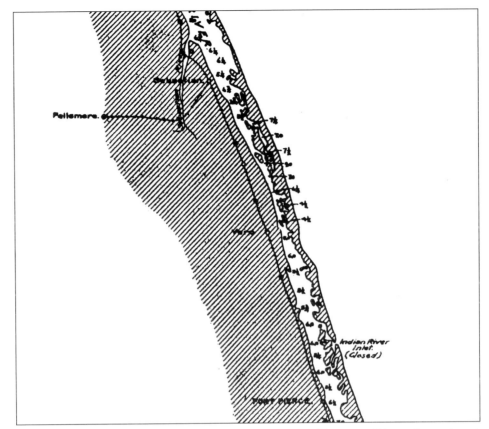

seasonal visitors represented a substantial source of income. River channel and inlet improvements, like highway construction, would encourage tourism, boating, and fishing. Consequently, after successful lobbying by Indian River County residents and officials, the U.S. Army Corps of Engineers renewed its efforts to improve navigation access through the inlets between the barrier islands separating the ocean from the mainland. Since the 1870s, commercial shippers had braved shallow shifting inlets. Tidal action had defeated previous attempts to widen and deepen the places of entry, quickly filling them with sand and making navigation uncertain and dangerous. Before the twentieth century, water travelers along Florida's east coast made their way through a broken series of lagoons, haulovers, and inlets. Local cries for improvements were generally resisted by federal engineers, who believed such projects too costly for the projected benefits.

Consequently, the first significant improvements to the river channel came from the private sector. Organized in 1881, the Florida Coast Line Canal & Transportation Company (FCLC&TC) reached an agreement with the state that gave the company 3,840 acres of public lands for each mile of canal it constructed. Dredging began in 1883 and by 1890 the company's general manager, George F. Miles, reported completion of a channel through the Indian River that was five feet deep and fifty feet wide at mean low water. The FCLC&TC claimed to have made twenty-three cuts across shoals between Titusville and Jupiter Inlet. The work earned the business over a half a million acres in granted lands. Although the company met the minimum threshold of its agreement, the Corps of Engineers found its work wanting and the navigation improvements marginal.

Spurred by Senator Matthew Quay, whose summer home lay along the route, the Corps in 1894 took over dredging along a seventy-seven mile stretch of the Indian River between Goat Creek, north of St. Sebastian River in Brevard County, and Jupiter Inlet. The *Suwannee* began scooping the river bottom in July at a place called "Long Cut," thirteen miles north of Fort Pierce. Additional dredging at "High Bank Canal," three miles farther north, moved 11,000 cubic yards of material, much of which washed back into the canal in the wakes of passing steamboats. In 1908, the chief of engineers reported "The improvement has had no effect upon freight rates. The commerce of Indian River is small. The waterway is used only by launches, small local steamers, and sailing vessels." With the exception of the Goat Creek-to-Jupiter Inlet stretch of waterway, the Corps took no other part in local dredging.

The FCLC&TC completed its work in 1912. Extending 3,650 miles from the mouth of the St. Johns River to Biscayne Bay, the channel had a nominal width of fifty feet and a depth of five feet. Irregular maintenance of the channel caused continuing problems with navigation, however. The channel still did not safely accommodate small boats. Colonel William Craighill of the Corps, who favored federal control of dredging operations, noted that the *St. Lucie,* a 120-foot steamer weighing 165 tons and capable of carrying 130 passengers, had difficulty navigating the Indian River. Passengers experienced delays because the ship often ran aground on sand banks.

Not until 1927 did the canal company and the federal government come to terms on control of the waterway. In that year, the Congress created the Florida Inland Navigation District (FIND) and authorized it to purchase the waterway. Commissioners from the state's eleven east coast counties made up the FIND board of directors, who had authority to tax and issue bonds. In 1929, FIND acquired the rights-of-way to the Indian River. Vero Beach's Axel Peterson served as Indian River County's FIND representative during the 1930s. Renewed dredg-

These photographs, dating between 1919 and the late 1930s, tell a story of the tenacity of Sebastian's early settlers in dealing with the treacherous inlet. Heavy rainfalls and shifting currents hampered efforts to develop a stable inlet channel and eroded the foundations of many cabins built there.

ing resulted in the completion in 1935 of a continuous channel between Jacksonville and Miami 120 feet wide and 8 feet deep. The federal government stopped common-carrier freight service along the waterway during the war, a crippling blow to the industry, one from which it never truly recovered. By 1950, Florida's Intracoastal Waterway supported nearly 10,000 recreational craft, but only a handful of contract commercial shippers. New projects to dredge the channel to 12 feet and widen it to 125 feet were unveiled in the 1950s. By then, $13 million had been expended on channel improvements.

The Corps also dredged tributary channels from the Intracoastal Waterway into Sebastian and Vero Beach. In 1937, the Corps recommended an entrance channel 120 feet wide and 8 feet deep with a turning basin, extending from the main waterway and terminating north of downtown Sebastian. Commerce on the waterway had jumped from 145,000 tons to 532,000 tons between 1928 and 1937. Still, pleasure craft dominated river traffic. Sebastian residents believed that a tributary channel, small basin, terminal facility, and inlet improvements would encourage boaters to tie up there and thus promote the local economy. During World War II, trainees from the U.S. Navy's underwater demolition team (UDT) based in Fort Pierce blasted shoals at Sebastian Inlet, but the materials eventually worked their way back into low areas, leaving the channel virtually unchanged. Vero Beach actually did get a turning basin, thanks to the Corps. Encouraged by that development, the Vero Beach Yacht Club, incorporated in 1926, was reorganized. In 1937, the new yacht club acquired a site in the Veromar subdivision north of the municipal dock, where it eventually built its own docks and clubhouse.

Local agricultural production continued to expand during the Depression. Despite its relatively small size, Indian River County in 1934 stood nineteenth nationwide in grapefruit shipments and the state's sixth most productive citrus county. Additionally, by 1936 county farmers were tilling nearly 1,800 acres of vegetables. Most farms were owner-operated, although managers supervised the operations of a small number of large farms. Tenancy and sharecropping played small roles in the region's agricultural heritage. Only forty-one tenant farmers were recorded in the 1930s and most of them paid cash to plow fields on Indian River County farms. Only one sharecropper was recorded.

As their groves expanded and fruit sales became more competitive, Florida's growers adopted decorative and colorful crate labels as part of their marketing strategy. In bright colors, the labels displayed such themes as animals, flowers, humor, patriotism, royalty, songs, and various exotic subjects. Images of women

The Graves Brothers Citrus Packing House, 1936. In the late-1920s and 1930s, the Graves brothers planted hundred of acres of citrus in Indian River County.

provided a popular theme, portraying Southern belles as guardians of truth and symbols of beauty or even displaying short-skirt flappers and the "come hither" girls of the 1930s. Pin-up girls appeared on some labels. W.G. Roe's 1932 "Blue Lake" label featured a topless Indian female, while Fred Johnston's risque "Nudist" label even appeared in *Esquire Magazine*, the boldest journal of the times. The "Flo" brand used by Indian River packers and growers was more restrained in its depiction of women, picturing them in fashionable swimming suits. The citrus labels that appeared in the twenty years or so before World War Two reflected the changes that occurred in fashion and hair style.

Competition for customer recognition reached feverish proportions in the Depression, compelling the Florida Citrus Commission in 1937 to register crate labels. By 1941, a host of labels adorned citrus crates shipped from Indian River County. Graves Brothers, Oslo Citrus Growers Association, Indian River Associates, and Vero Indian River Producers Association shared the rights to the "Flo," "Florigold," "Justice," and "Tasteit" brand labels. Joseph S. Earman Farms, Inc. of Vero Beach used the "Ace Flite," "Par Flite," and "Top Flite" brands. A native of Jacksonville, Florida, Earman had graduated from Cornell University in 1925 and published the *Palm Beach Independent* until 1930. About 1932, he moved to Vero Beach, where he organized the Indian River Citrus Bank and the Vero Beach Ice and Storage Company.

The "Anco," "Junco," and "Sonco" labels advertised the citrus of the W.J. Orth Packing Company. The Rosbottom & Waker Company of Vero Beach advertised their produce with the "Vero Maid" label. Axel Peterson moved to Vero Beach in 1914 from

The Exposition Building and Community Hall was completed in 1938. It housed the annual county fair, which included displays of Indian River citrus. The building later served as the Elk's Lodge clubhouse.

Moline, Illinois and began cultivating lime trees. By the 1930s, his packing house shipped citrus crates displaying the "Athedor," "Honey Dew," and "Lundeen" labels. "Chief Sleepy Eye," "Chief Scarlet Feather," and "Chief Purple Feather" of Indian River Products, Inc. and Indian River Fruit & Vegetable Distributors played on the county's name. Deerfield Groves Company used, among other labels, "Flint," "Indian Deer," and "Orchid." Another Vero Beach packer, Jack Napier Strong, shipped grapefruit under the "Jungle Garden" label. Other labels registered to Indian River County citrus shippers included "Autocrat," "Checkers," "Heart," "Hi-Hat," "Moonsmile," "Oslo," "Sachem," "Selco," and "Wabasso." In the 1950s, shippers turned to frozen concentrate orange juice and printed corrugated cardboard boxes, bringing an end to an era of decorative citrus crate labels.

Near Fellsmere, sugar cane fields replaced orange groves. Cane growing became a big business in Florida after World War I, and the state's growers soon stripped Louisiana of its "sugar bowl" mantle. Congressman S. Wallace Dempsey

The Fellsmere Sugar Company promoted growth in Indian River County during the Great Depression. This aerial scene depicts the plant at its high point of production in the mid-1950s.

boasted in 1927 that "Sugar cane is now being grown to a greater height and large sugar content than any other area of the world and better than in the Island of Cuba." The Lake Okeechobee region contained the largest operations, managed by Chicago-based Celotex and the Pennsylvania Sugar Company. In its drive to match crops and resources with the location of raw materials, Depression-era Florida was fatally attracted to low-wage industries.

Indian River growers had experimented with large-scale sugar cane operations for over thirty years. Despite recurrent floods, a Fellsmere sugar producers association, organized in 1914, produced a consistent flow of cane syrup. At Vero Beach, the Steam Syrup Company, operated by McVay Lindsay & Sons, installed a syrup mill in 1921. The five-reel crusher mill was capable of grinding eighty tons of cane daily. A forty-five horsepower stationary steam engine propelled the machinery, which squeezed processed cane juice into syrup. Although the business eventually failed, ten years later a new large-scale sugar operation at Fellsmere appeared, bringing renewed hope to the economically-ravaged farming community.

Business conditions around Fellsmere actually improved somewhat during the Depression. The Fellsmere Sugar Company, fast becoming one of Florida's largest sugar producers, offered a source of employment. Organized by Frank Heiser, William Douglas, Maurice Leonard, J.O. Roberts, and E.V.R. Thayer, the company improved the drainage system, cleared fields, and planted cane fields. General manager Heiser worked with a shoestring budget to install a grinding mill, which was assembled from a former muck plant, and other equipment imported from Cuba and Louisiana. The mill operations and 1,400 acres of cane in 1933 provided jobs for over 200 residents, all but eliminating local unemployment rolls.

Fellsmere muck yielded 2 million pounds of raw sugar in the company's first season. The company shipped its product out of state for refining until 1935, when it installed a refinery, the first in the state. The Winn-Lovett Company food chain marketed the refined sugar under the "Florida Crystals" trademark throughout the

Waldo Sexton, one of Indian River County's most colorful residents, helped develop the resort image of Vero Beach in the 1930s.

Waldo Sexton's unique Driftwood Inn, shown here in the 1940s, was assembled in part from flotsam collected along the shores of the Atlantic Ocean. The Driftwood began as Sexton's beachside four-room summer house. By 1935, when opened to the public, the building had been transformed into a two-story, rambling hostelry. The rustic beachcomber Driftwood is listed in the National Register of Historic Places and now supports an expanded Driftwood Resort complex.

eastern seaboard. Several years later, Fellsmere Sugar Company reorganized into Fellsmere Sugar Producers Association. It refined nearly 7 million pounds in 1938, leading the *Vero Beach Press-Journal* to predict that Fellsmere sugar "may make the Indian River section as famous for sugar as it now is for citrus." By then, most Florida sugar came from fields and factories owned by a few large well-financed growers working in close cooperation with the U.S. Sugar Corporation. Puerto Rican businessmen purchased the Fellsmere Association's property and trademark in 1943. Eventually, Gulf & Western Corporation acquired the property and converted the fields to orange groves. Thus ended the era of sugar production in Indian River County.

Two men who during the era left their mark on Indian River County were Waldo Sexton and Arthur G. McKee. Sexton, a native of Indiana and a 1911 graduate of Purdue University, bought a farm west of Vero in 1914 and organized the Indian River Products Company. It was the first of many real estate and citrus companies which with Sexton was involved. He sold $2 million worth of real estate in the 1920s and by 1935 was annually exporting thousands of boxes of citrus from his 800 acres of groves. His dairy farm introduced the Guinea cow to the region, and he cross-bred Brahman and White Shorthorn cows to develop a breed more resistant to Florida's heat and pests. His showplace dairy supplied milk to residents and, later, to servicemen at Vero Beach Naval Air Station.

Characterized as an "imaginative entrepreneur" and "outrageous, old-time eccentric," Sexton contributed to the resort image of Vero Beach with the Driftwood Inn. Assembled in part from flotsam collected along the shores of the Atlantic Ocean, the Driftwood began as Sexton's beachside four-room summer house. By 1935, it had become a two-story, rambling hotel. Sexton personally supervised the organic development of what one writer called "the damnedest place you ever saw." Rustic, earthy, and open to the ocean breezes, the "Driftwood rises out of the sea," in Sexton's words. With an architecture that could only be described as "rustic beachcomber," the Driftwood was deceptively modern in its appointments. The ground-floor focal point was a central breezeway occupied by a large mahogany main table, a remnant of the St. Louis World's Fair. Much of the inn's furniture was crafted from walnut and mahogany logs cast upon the shore. Even the signs advertising the inn along the streets of Vero Beach were crafted from driftwood. Listed in the National Register of Historic Places, the Driftwood Inn and Hotel now supports an expanded Driftwood Resort complex.

One of Sexton's business partners and a seasonal resident, Arthur G. McKee first visited Vero Beach in 1922. He built a seasonal home at Riomar. A graduate of Pennsylvania State University, he founded Arthur G. McKee & Co. in Cleveland in 1915 and achieved international recognition as an engineer and inventor. He held numerous patents in steel manufacturing. McKee built Steel plants in Brazil, India, and Russia. Specializing in the manufacture of blast furnaces, McKee's company had completed 2,500 projects in 42 counties by 1956, generating sales of 1 billion dollars, a fabulous sum at the time.

McKee's "second great enterprise," McKee Jungle Gardens, was constructed south of Vero Beach. In his travels, McKee had developed an interest in tropical plant culture, which he translated into the garden-jungle attraction. Launched in 1925, the gardens occupied eighty acres that his cousin, Charles McKee, had purchased in the 1910s. Sexton became the manager and director of the project. In 1930, McKee hired William Lyman Phillips, a pioneer of tropical landscape architecture, to design the placement of the garden's pathways, creeks, plants, and trees. A quiet, self-effacing man, Phillips profoundly influenced Florida landscape design in the 1920s and 1930s, helping to landscape estates at Mountain Lake Colony and Bok Tower Gardens in Lake Wales and Fairchild Tropical Garden in Miami. He often worked on projects with Frederick Law Olmstead, Jr., who considered Fairchild Garden "a masterful piece of work." Younger landscape architects then practicing in the state considered Phillips the dean of Florida landscape architecture.

Phillips and McKee introduced plants from six continents to the Jungle Gardens, including over 100 varieties of palm trees and 40 types of rubber and other tropical plants. Phillips had characteristically hacked his way through many overgrown settings to create picturesque landscape designs, which often served as a backdrop to buildings and structures. After visiting the McKee Jungle Gardens, May Mann Jennings, the wife of a former Florida governor and a leading advocate of women's rights and conservation, implored Phillips to use the same type of creeks he had sculpted at McKee for Royal Palm Park, which the Civilian Conservation Corps (CCC) was then constructing on Paradise Key in southern Dade County. Primates and reptiles from throughout the world contributed to the jungle atmosphere of McKee Jungle Gardens. McKee poured $100,000 into the attraction in its first decade, employing thirty people to maintain the animals, plants, and trees. The gardens formally opened in 1931 and within two decades attracted some 30,000 visitors annually.

To cushion the depression, the administration of Franklin Delano Roosevelt developed a series of relief programs, many of which passed through local government. Under the umbrella name of the "New Deal," the so-called "alphabet" programs, named for the acronyms assigned to them, helped counties and municipalities to improve infrastructure, construct buildings, conserve natural resources, and create recreational facilities. Such programs included the Works Progress Administration (WPA), Civil Works Administration (CWA), Civilian Conservation Corps (CCC), and Federal Emergency Relief Administration (FERA). The New Deal financed many projects in Indian River County during the 1930s. The county and city constructed sidewalks, parks, and streets and installed water and sewer lines. In 1935 alone, New Deal programs supported twenty-five projects in the county, including the removal of spoil banks in Vero Beach and the improvement of airstrips at Fellsmere and Sebastian.

Construction of the Indian River County Courthouse, completed through the assistance of the Public Works Administration (PWA), constituted the era's largest public construction project locally. Conceived early in the history of the PWA, the courthouse was one of the earliest large federally-financed projects in Florida. The application, submitted to the PWA in August 1933, called for construction to be financed through a $75,000 loan. The terms required the county to pay back only 70 percent of the amount it borrowed. The request

This photograph of the Indian River County Courthouse appeared in an official 1939 publication illustrating significant projects completed by the Works Progress Administration.
The upper photograph shows Clerk of Court Douglas Baker, standing to the right. Seated are Lelia Gray, Wanda Smith, and Ralph Harris at work in the building, about 1940.

obtained federal approval after intensive lobbying by local attorney and president of the Vero Beach Chamber of Commerce James T. Vocelle and Congressman J. Mark Wilson. After nearly eighteen months of negotiating, the PWA approved the loan in February 1935.

The City of Vero Beach donated a site for the courthouse on 14th Avenue (Seminole Avenue opposite Pocahontas Park. Voters approved a bond issue to raise the financial collateral against the federal loan. The county enlisted architect William Garns to design the new courthouse. Garns had first visited Vero Beach at the height of the land boom, but returned to his Indianapolis practice in 1927. In 1933 he abandoned his native home for Vero Beach, where he took up permanent residency. A prolific designer of buildings, Garns also designed Vero Beach's First Baptist Church, the Community Building, and several large, fashionable houses in Vero Beach and Riomar.

Contractor William Hensick & Son supervised the building's construction. A contractor since 1925, Hensick assembled many of the fashionable houses that Garns designed. Among them was a sprawling $27,000 mansion for J.M. Hopwood of Pittsburg on Osceola Boulevard (S.R.60) and the Reed Hutchison House in McAnsh Park. In March 1937, as Hensick was installing the finishing touches on

Community Building in Pocahontas Park, Vero Beach, Florida V-19

The Vero Beach Community Building

As the courthouse arose, construction also proceeded across the street on the Vero Beach Community Building. And it too was designed by architect William Garns and built by workers furnished by the Federal Emergency Relief Administration (FERA) agency and the Union Workers Association of Vero Beach. Dedicated on July 4, 1935, the wood-frame-and-stucco-building cost a mere $3,650. The Modern Woodmen of America sponsored the dedication, which included a concert by the Lake Worth boy's band, a dance, and a ballgame between the Vero Beach and West Palm Beach teams of the East Coast Baseball League. During World War II, the building functioned as an entertainment center for servicemen. Many couples met there for the first time. Perhaps no other building in Vero Beach holds an equal place in the memories and hearts of residents. Located at 2140 Fourteenth Avenue, the building is listed in the National Register of Historic Places and currently houses the Indian River Citrus Museum.

the courthouse, Garns died. While speaking to the Vero Beach Rotary Club, Garns indicated he was feeling ill and then collapsed into the lap of Harry Jones, the club president. He never regained consciousness. His courthouse was one of only eleven buildings in Florida that the PWA selected to illustrate a book on its projects, which it published to showcase its program and silence New Deal critics.

Across the street from the courthouse the Vero Beach Community Building underwent concurrent design and development. After Garns completed the plans in January 1935, labor was furnished by the Federal Emergency Relief Administration (FERA) agency and the Union Workers Association of Vero Beach. Originally measuring ninety by forty-two feet, the wood-frame-and-stucco-building cost $3,650 to construct and was dedicated on July 4, 1935. The Modern Woodmen of America sponsored the event, which included a concert by the Lake Worth boy's band, a dance, and a ballgame between the Vero Beach and West Palm Beach teams of the East Coast Baseball League. Containing a main assembly room, stage, and wings at both ends of the structure, the Community Building became a popular location of various social activities.

The New Deal also funded archaeological investigations. Under sponsorship by the CWA, two sites were excavated near Cape Canaveral in 1933. P.D McKellar found a bed of fossils near Winter Beach in 1936 and, later, another near Gifford. Charles Higgs, a seasonal resident from Wisconsin, explored a site on the peninsula north of the Narrows and found what he believed to be "the seat of native Ais wrecking operations." Higgs collected cannons and Spanish colonial artifacts that he found near the beach, along with considerable evidence that treasure hunters had preceded him. That important discovery later attracted anthropologist Hale G. Smith of the Florida Park Service to the county. Their efforts contributed to the eventual listing in the National Register of Historic Places of the Spanish Fleet & Salvors Camp Site.

The *Vero Beach Press-Journal* began its second decade of publication during the Great Depression. The *Press-Journal* building in Vero Beach received a face-lift in 1937, becoming the first International style structure in Indian River County, a streamline design that broke away from tradition to emphasize futuristic concepts. The newspaper descended from two separate newspapers. The first, the *Vero Press,* was organized in March 1919 by Tom Campbell and Paul Nisle. About 1913, Nisle had helped establish the *Marion County Advocate* in Dunnellon, Florida, but left six years later for the east coast. The *Vero Press* employed several headmasts in its earliest editions, including "A Paper With A

In this 1930 photograph, James Tew, president of B.F. Goodrich Rubber Company, poses beside his company plane at Vero Beach Airport. The Goodrich Silvertowns logo stenciled on the fuselage refers to the name of a subsidiary organized in 1928 to manage Goodrich's service stations and retail outlets.

Heart and Soul, Devoted Exclusively To The People" and "Vero-Where the Tropics Begin."

Campbell and Nisle's *Vero Press* remained the only local newspaper until the *Vero Beach Journal* published its first issue in December 1925. Under the headmast "The People's Paper," the *Journal* was organized by J. Clemment Brossier, Robert Brossier, and John F. Schumann. Native to Key West, the Brossiers abandoned their Miami newspaper businesses in 1914 for Orlando, where they purchased the Reporter-Star Publishing Company. Attorney John Schumann, editor and part-owner, arrived in Orlando in 1910. Schumann had previously managed newspapers in Frankfort, Indianapolis, and Toledo. Tireless in his pursuit of advertising and news, he edited the *Morning Sentinel,* then bought into and edited the *Melbourne Times-Journal,* and eventually took over a third paper in Lakeland. In 1925, while maintaining his connections with those three newspapers, he began publishing a fourth newspaper in Vero Beach. His son, John J. Schumann, a graduate of Indiana University's law school, eventually took over the Vero Beach paper. In 1927, Schumann, a relative newcomer in the community, purchased the *Journal* and consolidated the names of the two newspapers to form the *Vero Beach Press-Journal.* With a local newspaper monopoly, he increased the annual subscription rate from two to three dollars.

Eastern Air Lines initiated commercial service in 1932, using Vero Beach's airfield for refueling stops. Eastern increased its presence there three years later, when it instituted passenger and air mail flights on its "Great Silver Fleet." Twelve hundred people assembled at the airport in October 1935 for the first flight, which carried out of Indian River County nearly fifty-five hundred letters.

Schumann's weekly *Press-Journal* successfully weathered the lean years of the Depression. Late in the decade, his hard work and vision gained the business awards of excellence. Annual special editions increased in size from twenty-eight pages in 1934 to forty-two pages in 1937. The newspaper often used half-tone images associated with the resurgent building trades, and it consistently extolled the benefits of living in Indian River County. In 1939, the Florida State Press Association gave the *Press-Journal* its John C. Lochman Award as the best weekly newspaper in Florida.

The county's first airport, near Vero Beach, was dedicated in March 1930. The ceremony included an appearance by a Goodyear dirigible, arranged with the help of James Tew, president of B.F. Goodrich Company and a seasonal resident of Riomar. Bud Holman, owner of a local automobile dealership, served as the airport manager. Commercial service began in 1932, when Eastern Air Lines began using the airfield for refueling stops. Eastern expanded its presence three years later when it instituted passenger and air mail flights from Vero Beach. The first such flight, which departed October 18, 1935, drew a crowd of 1,200 onlookers and flew away with nearly 5,500 locally posted letters.

Vero Beach Airport, December 10, 1935. This scene of the city's airport was snapped during the Army Air Corps's Florida war games. Two hundred planes participated in maneuvers that included thirty Martin bombers, which flew mock raids from Vero Beach to "destroy" docks and ships at Biscayne Bay and Tampa Bay.

A growing awareness of the effectiveness of air power as a weapon of war and the gathering of war clouds in Europe precipitated in the mid-1930s efforts to attract a military presence to the county. Several Florida cities, Jacksonville, in particular, sent resolutions to the President and the Congress urging the construction of coastal air defenses along the nation's long, vulnerable coastline. Many residents of Indian River County, notably Vero Beach's indefatigable airport manager, Bud Holman, wanted to be part of that system.

Their efforts were rewarded in December 1935, when the Army Air Corps chose the Vero Beach field as a host site for its war games. In all, 200 planes participated in the Florida maneuvers, half of them stationed at Vero Beach. Holman arranged for improvements to the airport, such as permanent lighting of the runways and the installation of radios and teletype machines. The fifteen-day exercise began on December 1, 1935, when thirty Martin bombers and their crews arrived from Langley Field, Virginia, and Riverside and Hamilton Fields, California. General H.H. "Hap" Arnold, later the famed wartime chief of the Army Air Corps, commanded the Vero Beach squadron. Over the space of two weeks, mock raids from Vero Beach "destroyed" docks and ships at Biscayne Bay and Tampa Bay. The brief interruption of civilian service at the Vero Beach airport presaged a much longer and more intensive experience five years later. In 1939, using WPA labor, the city expanded the field's runways. The following year, as a national defense measure, the Civilian Aviation Administration poured an additional quarter million dollars into the facility.

Despite enjoying a relatively bright local economy, one that most areas of the nation might have envied in the Depression Era, Indian River County did not entirely escape the financial wrath of the times. Many properties went into receivership, their owners unable to meet mortgage obligations. The Vero Del Mar hotel complex, completed in 1926 at a cost of $250,000, sold at the courthouse steps for $25,000 in 1930. Hardly a decade old, the Vero Theater was acquired in 1936 by Veebee Theater Corporation of Fort Pierce for $50,000, which promptly spent $25,000 to upgrade the building, making it "the largest lighted marquee in Florida." Richard Treadway and partner John Wriston purchased the Royal Park Inn at a fire-sale price of $49,500 in 1937. Three-foot-high weeds and a dank, musty interior revealed to the New England hotel owners that the building had remained vacant for some years. They immediately imported furniture and employees from their New England hotels and scratched for business. Treadway once recalled that in the late 1930s he often stood along U.S.

NAS Vero Beach officially existed between November 1942 and March 1946. These views illustrate some of the infrastructure and aircraft at NAS Vero Beach during World War II. The main hangar and tower were products of Detroit architect Albert Kahn and the U. S. Navy's Bureau of Yards and Docks. Personnel trained in various aircraft, including Buccaneers, Hellcats, Helldivers, and Tigercats.

Highway 1 handing out brochures to passing motorists.

The saga of Vero Beach's Royal Park Arcade epitomized the tragic circumstances of the era. The Vero Beach Construction Company, lacking sufficient capital to continue its construction operations, had halted construction of the Twenty-first Street hotel in February 1926. Later that year, receivers Freeman Knight and William Atkin appointed contractor J. Hudson Baker to resume work on the building, which was completed in December 1926. Despite generating some revenues, the property remained in receivership until 1930, when the Nevada Investment Company of Palm Beach County purchased it. Six weeks later, Frederick S. Ruth, a wealthy New York City realtor, acquired the property.

By that time, Ruth stood atop a national real estate firm, whose operations he directed from lavish offices on Broadway Avenue in New York City. He served as president and director of Chocomount Homes, Inc., the Mountain Lakes Corporation in Florida, and the Whippoorwill Corporation. He also served as a director of Fishers Island Corporation, Northern Capital Corporation, and the Florida Citrus Exchange. It was in the course of developing Mountain Lake near Lake Wales, where construction began in 1914, that Ruth became aware of Vero Beach. He plunged deeply into real estate there and elsewhere throughout the state and managed to survive the collapse of the Florida Boom. But the stock market crash in October 1929 brought ruin to his financial empire. Despondent and unable to rally his businesses, Ruth committed suicide in his Waldorf-Astoria apartment in 1932.

World War II, the climactic event of the twentieth century, a great divide in American history, lifted the nation out of the Depression. The war brought great economic and social changes to Indian River County, like every other part of the

Garnett Lunsford Radin

The financial stress of managing a hospital in the throes of the Great Depression of the 1930s burns brightest in Garnett Lunsford Radin's memory of early life in Indian River County. After receiving her nursing certificate from the Nebraska Methodist Hospital in 1926, she returned to Vero Beach. As the county grew, Nurse Radin joined Dr. E. Bacon Hardee and Charles Ervin (Cephus) Cox, a funeral director, in seeking a location for a new hospital. The new facility, a two-story tourist home on Dixie Highway south of the city limits of Vero Beach, opened May 12, 1932. Every room had hot and cold running water. Patients paid $5.50 a day for a private room and $4.50 for a shared room. The price included food and nursing care. Three nurses from Nebraska arrived to help Nurse Radin. Each received a monthly salary of $70.

Indian River County's first hospital opened in 1932.

A WWII Navy dispensary building served as the second county hospital from 1948-1952.

At the height of the depression, many patients paid their hospital bills with fruit and vegetables. Nurse Radin leased the hospital to a non-profit group in 1942, when she joined the U.S. Navy and went to war, along with millions of other service men and women.

The medical building at the Naval Air Station became the county hospital after World War II. A new building on 25th Street was constructed in the 1950s. It is now the county administration building. The present hospital between Indian River Boulevard and U.S. 1 was erected in the 1980s.

country. In 1942, the U.S. Navy notified Vero Beach officials that it had selected their municipal airport as the site for a naval air station. After reaching an agreement with city officials, the Navy purchased 1,500 additional acres surrounding the facility and closed several streets to local traffic. The plans for Naval Air Station Vero Beach, or NAS Vero Beach as it was officially designated, were developed by the Bureau of Yards and Docks (BYD) in June 1942. Wasting no time, the Hillyer and Lovan Construction Company of Jacksonville set up an office in the Vero Del Mar and began work in July. By August, 1,200 workers were building runways and assembling buildings, which included an armory, barracks, a control tower, a landplane hangar, an assembly and repair shop, magazines, and warehouses. The base was formally commissioned in November 1942. By 1945, the U.S. Navy maintained eighty naval air stations in the continental United States. The station at Vero Beach complemented a series of such bases located at Daytona Beach, DeLand, Fort Lauderdale, Melbourne, Lake City, Sanford, and Brunswick, Georgia. Strategically placed along the east coast, those stations served as satellite fields to the main facilities at Jacksonville, Key West, and Miami. NAS Vero Beach had its own satellite base, a small field at Roseland, completed in 1942. By the war's end in 1945, additional fields at Stuart and Fort Pierce provided support to NAS Vero.

Most buildings at the Florida's naval air stations employed wood frame structural systems. The majority of them, so-called "Theater of Operations Buildings," also designated as "temporary" or "mobilization" by the military, were assembled from standardized plans prepared by the War Department during World War I. The drawings, unchanged since the end of that conflict, became the basis for many World War II buildings. The long, rectangular buildings were adopted by the Navy Department for its cantonments. Buildings unique to the base at NAS Vero and other stations were designed by the Navy's Bureau of Yards and Docks (BYD). For its largest and most unusual projects—aircraft hangars, power houses, and torpedo workshops—the Navy turned to professional architects and engineers, such as Robert & Company of Atlanta and Albert Kahn of Detroit. Kahn's "all-under-one-roof" industrial manufacturing concept and his "all-on-one-floor" design provided the basis for postwar mass housing construction.

Irene Harms Nelson

Irene Harms Nelson recalls a very wet rainy season in 1924 when she moved with her family from Tallahassee to the Indian River region, where her father went to work for the Graves Brothers. The 350-mile trip took three days. Her father soon purchased a grocery store, which failed during the Great Depression of the 1930s, she said, because "he let people have food on credit and they didn't pay." Mr. Harms returned to work for the Graves Brothers Farm and remained with the company forty years.

Pilot training at NAS Vero Beach began in February 1943. Six concrete runways laced the airport, the longest of them stretching 6,100 feet. Trainees initially flew the ill-fated Brewster Buccaneer, despised for its slow speed and lack of maneuverability. Later, NAS Vero Beach pilots practiced night fighting in Grumman F6F Hellcats. One pilot later commented that "We would fly all night, and then we would fly all the next day looking for the guys who didn't come back the night before." Many never returned. Ensign David Proudman and Ensign Lemuel Harrison lost their lives in November 1944 while on "routine training missions" over the Atlantic Ocean. In all, nearly 100 pilots died while training at NAS Vero Beach.

At its peak of activity, NAS Vero Beach held 1,400 servicemen and 250 planes. A station newspaper, *The Buccaneer*, published news of local activities and national events. The Community Building in Pocahontas Park was expanded and converted into a United Service Center (USO), a civilian place for servicemen to gather in their off-duty hours. It suffered damage from a fire on November 2, 1944, but was at once repaired. The Bombadears, a Vero Beach social group, provided entertainment for the service men, many of whom considered the Community Building their "foster home." Service women were quartered at the Beachland Hotel and the Sebastian Inn. Some military personnel found housing at Vero Beach's Royal Park Inn, the Parkway Inn, and the Blue Lantern Inn. After the war ended the station was reduced to a skeleton staff. The Navy closed NAS Vero Beach in March 1947, returning it to its civilian owner.

The war engaged virtually every citizen. No one could escape material shortages of every conceivable item of goods or foods. The nation devoted its energies and efforts fully to winning the war. Meat, commodities such as sugar and coffee, and gasoline were closely rationed. Detroit produced only military vehicles. Communities held bond drives to finance the war effort. The Red Cross organized groups to prepare surgical dressings for military hospitals. Civilians staffed United Service Organization (USO) events, which provided entertainment for

---

Mary Studer

One of William Klecht's ten children, born in the first year of the new century, Mary moved with her father to a farm near Palm Bay in 1913, joining about a dozen other families in the area. Her father farmed, raising "whatever the season called for,"in Mary's words, recorded in 1988. Peppers, tomatoes, potatoes, beans, the "good crops if the price was right." But then if the price was right, every farmer in the area raised the same crops. "So you were always in debt." Mary attended a one-room school through the eighth grade and she wanted to attend high school in St. Augustine, taught by nuns, since the Klechts were strict Catholics. "Dad promised that when we had a good crop I could go. We never had a good crop," Mary recalled. She married in 1918, left the area, and did not return until 1956, when she settled in Vero Beach. Five of Mary Studer's sons were in military service during World War II. One, Robert, a pilot, did not return, listed as missing in action in the Pacific in the last month of the war.

servicemen and women stationed in the vicinity. The military reciprocated. Army musicians from Camp Blanding, near Starke, Florida, performed in concert at Pocahontas Park. The park often contained displays of weapons and equipment. One demonstration performed for civilians at Vero NAS involved men crawling under live machine-gun fire toward mock Japanese pillboxes.

At the end of the war in 1945, Indian River County embarked on an era of growth that was to continue throughout the rest of the century. Millions of servicemen and women from throughout the United States trained in Florida. Many returned afterward to make the state their home. Florida offered, at the time, wide expanses of undeveloped beachfront property that provided spectacular views of the Atlantic Ocean, inexpensive housing, relatively low property taxes, and, best of all, a warm climate. There was much empty space. The county's population numbered a mere 9,000 in 1945. Vero Beach, the largest municipality, contained but 3,600 residents; Wabasso 1,000. One technological achievement of the war, the development of frozen orange juice concentrate, revolutionized the citrus industry. But, though citrus groves continued to expand for the next thirty years and other businesses found a hospitable home in Indian River County, another industry, albeit a familiar one to Florida, tourism, came to dominate the economy and many aspects of life in the postwar state.

Chapter Seven
Postwar and Beyond:
The Time After World War II

AMERICA EMERGED FROM WORLD WAR II A WEALTHY NATION. In the half century of rising prosperity that followed, few states expanded as enthusiastically as Florida, which picked up where it had left off in 1926 after the post-World War I boom collapsed. The state's burgeoning population, growing wealth, and swelling economy in the next fifty years indelibly transformed the landscape and patterns of development within many of its counties. The citizens of Indian River County nevertheless resisted destructive change. While in other counties along the Atlantic oceanfront the pristine coastal line of vegetation gave way to high-rise condominiums and rows of houses, Indian River County retained a natural shoreline by restricting the height of structures and acquiring large expanses of oceanfront land.

Unlike many counties where urban dwellers abandoned towns and cities in favor of sprawling, gated communities, the towns and cities in Indian River County planned for organized growth. Throughout the state, the population growth, numbers of tourists, and growing reliance on the automobile resulted in wholesale construction of new highways. Along many of the major roadways favored by tourists, commercial development replaced historic architecture. Indian River County restricted commercial roadside "strip malls" to planned, designated intersections. The corridors between such commercial "nodes" provided a mixture of residential development and green space that made entrances into the county appealing and practical. The county's population growth revealed the need for such careful planning: The number of residents jumped nearly three-fold between 1945 and 1960 and doubled again by 1980. By the end of the century, over 100,000 people called Indian River County home.

The post-war era began in Indian River County with a celebrated event, the arrival of the Brooklyn Dodgers, who in 1948 opened a spring training camp at Vero Beach. One of America's most widely recognized professional baseball teams, closely followed by the powerful New York media, the Dodgers enjoyed a

Dodger manager Walter Alston places a Brooklyn Dodgers baseball cap on Florida Governor Leroy Collins. Flanking the Governor are Dodgers owner, Walter O'Malley, Florida State Senator Merrill Barber, and local businessman Bud Holman.

Heading for New York and the opening game of the 1949 World Series, Brooklyn Dodgers supporters from Vero Beach board Eastern Air Line's "Dodger Special." On the front row from the left are Luster Merriman, Dorabelle Holman, Fred Briggs, Jack Howard, Charles Toole, Jim Barrett, Allison Warren. Standing on the steps from the bottom are "Doc" Charlie McClure, Miles Warren, Bud Holman, John Schumann, Jr., John Schumann, Sr., Larry Maher, Jr., pilot Frank Bennett, and Bump Holman. The Dodgers had edged out the St. Louis Cardinals for the National League title, but would lose to another perennial contender, the New York Yankees, in the Fall Classic.

national constituency of fans. Beloved in part as baseball's inveterate losers, the Dodgers in 1948 comprised the only major league franchise that, despite numerous appearances, had never won the World Series. Renowned for their cross-town rivalry with the New York Giants and familiar victims of the New York Yankees in the Fall Classic, the Dodgers inspired fans to cry annually, "Wait Until Next Year." Following their defeat in the 1941 World Series at the hands of the Yankees, the Dodgers brought in Branch Rickey as general manager. A visionary businessman and shrewd judge of baseball talent, Rickey built a franchise second to none, pioneering the development of the farm system, scouts, and modern spring training camps. Rickey also changed American society when he brought into major league baseball the first African-American player, Jackie Robinson.

Rickey signed Robinson to a contract in 1946, but only after the death of baseball czar Kennesaw Mountain Landis, who had opposed integration. Rickey's bold initiative proved to be a critical step in the development of the nation's civil rights movement, in which Vero Beach thus played a role. Rickey selected Vero Beach for the Dodgers spring training camp, in part, because of its isolation from

Florida's urban centers. The general manager believed that the small-town atmosphere of Vero Beach would help players concentrate on baseball and encourage fans and writers to focus on the sport rather than race. Rickey's gamble to break the color line with a top black athlete paid off handsomely. Record crowds filled Ebbets Field in New York and in other ballparks. It also drew much national attention to Vero Beach.

Major league baseball teams had trained in Florida cities since 1888 and, by 1929, ten of sixteen clubs held training camps in the Sunshine state. A big business dominated by northern businessmen, major league baseball remained a segregated institution in the 1940s, despite the obvious presence of great talent in the professional Negro leagues. Accordingly, Red Barber, a native of Sanford, Florida, who worked as the radio announcer for the Dodgers in the 1940s, expressed astonishment when Rickey confidentially told him that the Dodgers had signed Robinson and intended to play the great African-American athlete.

Rickey's choice of Vero Beach for a training site may have been linked to Robinson's arrival on the scene. Rickey believed that racism was less prevalent in Vero Beach than most other places in the South. Florida, in fact, its heritage firmly rooted in southern traditions, remained highly segregated. African-American baseball players, like all people of their race, encountered discrimination not only in larger cities, such as Jacksonville and Tampa, but in small towns as well. Jackie Robinson aroused protests in Sanford during his first year in the Dodger farm system, while Jacksonville and DeLand closed their stadiums to the integrated Dodger farm team.

At the time, virtually no blacks lived within the corporate limits of Vero Beach. Baseball great Roy Campanella later recalled that "Mr. Rickey said there'd be no segregation at Vero Beach. But if you leave out Dodgertown, we were segregated everywhere." Other players saw Vero Beach "full of prejudice." One remembered that local blacks lived "huddled together in the tiny adjoining town of Gifford, which consisted of a movie house, a drugstore, a barber shop, and a pool hall." Nonetheless, as a result of the historic alliance between Robinson and Rickey, change came to America and to Vero Beach.

Opened in 1917, the Booker T. Washington subdivision occupied six blocks northwest of downtown Vero Beach. An early African-American neighborhood, the community contained churches, general stores, and dwellings by the late-1920s. Most residents worked in area citrus groves. Children attended school at Gifford. By World War II, when this updated Sanborn Company map was published, the Booker T. Washington neighborhood contained nearly 100 buildings.

A 109-acre tract at Vero Beach's former naval air station easily lent itself to conversion into a complex of ballfields and housing, dining, and exercise facilities. The site accommodated the professional team and its affiliated farm clubs. Unlike previous facilities, it contained far more than just a ballfield and dressing rooms. Its proximity to the airport permitted ballplayers to move easily between the landing strip and training camp without entering Vero Beach itself. Initially, two barracks accommodated the athletes. Expensive improvements prompted one writer later to marvel that "there is nothing in baseball that matches the factory the Brooklyn Dodgers operate at this training base." Indeed, Dodgertown was the first professional baseball training site in the nation that offered a comprehensive array of facilities, and it set a new standard for such complexes.

Florida's Governor Millard Caldwell threw out the first ball at the dedication ceremonies for Dodgertown, which were held March 30, 1948. Some 6,000 people, accompanied by baseball commissioner Albert B. "Happy" Chandler, attended the ceremonies. The game that followed featured the Dodgers and their Montreal Royals farm club. Jackie Robinson, who at the time was playing for the Royals, hit the second pitch over the left-field wall into a crowd of African-American fans. But, the Dodgers beat the Royals five to four. The first spring training season at Dodgertown commenced in March 1949. At that point, Vero Beach became the smallest city in the country to support a spring training site for major league baseball. Seven hundred players from the professional team and its farm clubs in Asheville, Ft. Worth, Greenville, Miami, Mobile, St. Paul, and Valdosta converged on Vero Beach for their training. Thirty-six spring training games were scheduled for the new field. In the opener, with Robinson now a member of the Dodger ballclub, a hometown crowd of 3,000 fans enjoyed an eleven-inning game, which the Dodgers won.

The stadium was renamed four years later, on March 11, 1953, as Holman Stadium, in honor of Bud Holman, the manager of the airport and a director of Dodgertown. At the dedication ceremony, Indian River County residents applauded Holman, who was credited with first approaching Branch Rickey about

This photograph of the former barracks at NAS Vero Beach was taken in September, 1948. It became part of Dodgertown, the spring training baseball camp for the Brooklyn Dodgers. The Dodgers opened their first spring training season at Dodgertown in March 1949. Within several years, new facilities replaced the barracks.

installing the team at Vero Beach. The jewel in the Dodgertown crown, the stadium was fashioned by civil engineer Emil Praeger of New York, whose designs of airports, docks, and parks had brought him international recognition. Praeger's plan for Dodgertown included a 5,000-seat stadium, landscaped with an outfield berm planted in royal palm trees. That unusual feature remained in the field of play until 1988, when a fence was installed around the outfield. The combination of a small-town atmosphere and big league dollars created an aura of success, and brought considerable recognition to the area. The Dodgers won National League pennants in 1949, 1952, and 1953 and finally captured a World Series title in 1955. Change came in 1957, when the team left Brooklyn and moved to Los Angeles, creating a new legion of fans in a distant part of the country, many of whom had never before heard of Vero Beach or Dodgertown. Still, Vero Beach residents remained unwavering in their support for the Dodgers, and even gained a minor league franchise of their own in 1980.

The $800,000 steel-and-concrete Merrill Barber Bridge was dedicated on March 18, 1951. This aerial scene contrasts the alignments of the 1920 and 1951 bridges, the former with its distinctive curve.

Dodgertown drew national attention to Vero Beach. As a New York City-based team, the Dodgers were closely covered by the *New York Times*, which during the training season carried columns about the team's surroundings in Vero Beach, such as the relatively inexpensive accommodations, Dodgertown, McKee Jungle Gardens, and the area's recreational opportunities. New York travel agent Bill Gimlich offered excursions from New York City to Vero Beach. Gimlich's packages included spring training games at Dodgertown, cruises along the Indian River, trips to Bok Tower in Lake Wales, and a tour of McKee Jungle Gardens. C. E. Wright of the *Times* predicted in 1951 that the new $800,000 steel-and-concrete Merrill Barber Bridge spanning the Indian River would place Vero Beach on the leading edge of Florida's emerging resort-town image.

The post-war expansion included the significant introduction of industry along the central Florida coast. Piper Aircraft arrived in Vero Beach in 1957. The company quickly installed a research and development center on the grounds of the former naval air station, not far from Dodgertown. A major national aircraft manufacturing company, Piper Aircraft selected Vero Beach for its newest plant because of the facilities associated with the old naval station and the good flying

weather that Florida's central east coast region offered. Founded in Pennsylvania in 1929 by William T. Piper, the company developed its legendary Piper Cub in the 1930s. He sold 5,600 Cubs to the U.S. Army during World War II for use in aerial photography, artillery spotting, medical evacuation, pilot training, and reconnaissance. Fondly nicknamed "flying Jeep" and "grasshopper," the Cub earned a reputation for its durability and ability to take off and land on even the most primitive of airstrips. The enterprising Piper soon became a spokesman for small private aircraft. The Cub's low cost and ease of operation earned Piper a reputation as the "Henry Ford of Aviation."

In January 1961, the company finished the addition of a 150,000-square foot facility, placing its administrative and manufacturing operations under one roof. Howard Piper, a son of William T. Piper, Jr., served as the general manager of the plant, which primarily manufactured Cherokee aircraft. By 1967, Piper's Vero

The arrival of Piper Aircraft in the late 1950s held out the promise of Vero Beach becoming an important manufacturing center. By 1967, Piper's Vero Beach facility had expanded to eleven acres, and employed over two thousand people. The aerial and interior views of Piper Aircraft's facilities illustrate the company's Vero Beach operation near the height of its development.

Beach facility had expanded to 11 acres, including a state-of-the-art turntable that measured 114 feet in diameter. Architect David Robison, a graduate of the University of Florida and an avid pilot, designed the facility, which drew national acclaim. Robison later drafted plans for Indian River Memorial Hospital, Vero Beach Airport, Miracle Mile Courtesy House, and Beachland School. Large investments like that made by the Piper Company, coupled with the design skills of gifted architects, promoted commercial and industrial expansion.

Although manufacturing brought jobs to Indian River County, no combination of post-World War II factors encouraged residential growth as much as mosquito control and air conditioning. Early efforts to ward off mosquitoes consisted of little more than fans made of palm fronds, smudge pots, and the installation of window and door screens. In his later years, former State Senator Merrill Barber fondly recounted the claim by early settlers that one could "take a quart can and swing it through the air anytime of day or night and catch a gallon of mosquitoes." Fans, screens, and smudges provided some protection, but only temporary relief and did not address the larger issues of comfort and health. A cottage industry of assembling mosquito palm fronds provided several residents with a small income. Other remedies proved more costly to humans than mosquitoes, such as smudges which, when left on the porch near the front door smoldering overnight, sometimes resulted in house fires.

Concern about the diseases carried by mosquitoes, such as malaria and yellow fever, prompted the Florida State Board of Health to begin in the 1920s to examine the question of controlling the pests. Raymond Turck, then the state health board officer, recommended that residents eliminate breeding areas in cisterns, rain barrels, ditches, and other man-made structures. Greater help came in 1925, when the Florida Legislature created the first mosquito control district in Indian River County. The legislature assigned the Board of Health the task of examining the benefits of draining wetlands and

> ## Merrill Barber & Merrill Barber Bridge
>
> The county's explosive postwar growth began in Vero Beach, in part, with the opening of the extension of Twenty-first Street eastward forming the "Miracle Mile." The accompanying dedication of the Merrill Barber Bridge in March 1951 further relieved traffic congestion. The bridge was named for one of Vero Beach's most prominent businessmen and politicians. Barber arrived with his family in 1913, attended the University of Florida, and established a grower's supply store in Vero Beach in 1935. He entered politics three years later. A director of the Indian River Citrus Bank, Barber was elected president of the bank in 1948 and served in the Florida Senate between 1955 and 1966.

filling in saltwater marshlands to eliminate breeding places. Too expensive to implement comprehensively, the study's findings resulted in few tangible results. Although ditch-draining programs during the New Deal launched a small-scale attack on mosquito infestation, it was not until the war and the introduction of DDT, a potent nerve poison, that an effective antidote to the swarming, biting pests was found. And, in the long run, the true result of that antidote's application remains unknown.

Developed in Germany in the 1870s, DDT became Florida's first comprehensive mosquito control agent. U.S. military forces sprayed the poison liberally over jungle islands in the Pacific that they occupied in World War II. The commanding officer at NAS Vero Beach, Capt. Edwin R. Peck, ordered its use in Indian River County toward the close of the war when supplies of the poison became available for domestic use. A small biplane sprayed the chemical over the central east Florida landscape. Residents found that the poison indeed brought relief from the pesky insects. The Indian River Mosquito Control District assumed responsibility for spraying operations after the war, dispatching an army of small trucks equipped with fogging units to cast clouds of insecticide along canals, wetlands, and streets. It continued use of the poison until the early 1970s, when the harmful effects of DDT were widely recognized and the poison banned under federal law. The local control agencies then turned their efforts to controlling egg and larvae development, often using a dike-and-flooding process, spraying the Paris Green chemical, and by coating the watery breeding grounds of the insects with oil films.

Air conditioning and refrigeration also helped make Florida habitable for those unaccustomed to its long, steamy-hot summers. A nineteenth-century innovation, air conditioning was invented by Dr. John Gorrie of Apalachicola, who in the 1850s assembled the first mechanical refrigeration unit. After the Civil War, railroads introduced the so-called "refrigerated cars," ice-cooled and not mechanically refrigerated, to preserve meats and produce they transported to northern markets. Ice boxes appeared in the homes of the wealthy. In the early twentieth century, many communities, including Vero Beach, contained a plant for the manufacture of ice, and delivery men made daily rounds of residential neighborhoods, like postmen or milkmen, feeding the ice boxes cakes of cooling ice. Willis Carrier introduced the modern air conditioner in 1929 and within the decade a few of the homes of the very wealthy contained the machines. Not until after the war, however, did the use of air conditioning become widespread. Department stores and theaters were the usually the first institutions in a community to adopt climate control equipment. Central air conditioning became a standard feature of residential construction only in the 1960s.

Agriculture remained the backbone of the economy in post-war Indian River

Jackson Brothers

The Jackson family arrived in Wabasso in the early decades of the twentieth century. Theodore and Walter Jackson grew up in Wabasso, helping their father farm on the family homestead. Learning the citrus business while working for area growers, the Jacksons acquired land and planted their own groves after regular work days and on weekends. Soon they resigned from their regular jobs, and went into business together. Working as a team, the brothers repaired equipment, and fertilized, sprayed, and trimmed trees. Within several decades, their business included 200 acres of citrus trees, primarily marsh, pink, and red seedless grapefruit west of Wabasso and Winter Beach. Their diligent work, perseverance, and planning is part of a proud African-American legacy in Indian River County's agricultural history.

County, providing more employment than any other sector. In the 1990s, about 450 farms yielded nearly $250,000,000 in annual sales. The average farm contained 385 acres, but twenty of the county's farms were large spreads of greater than 2,000 acres. As late as 1997, some 250 farms with fewer than fifty acres each accounted for nearly 5,000 acres of the county's agriculture. Many farmers cultivated extensive citrus groves. Grapefruit alone accounted for 40,000 acres, plucked from nearly 4 million trees. The orange industry accounted for 31,000 acres and 3 million trees. In the last decade of the twentieth century, nearly one million pounds of grapefruit and 700,000 pounds of oranges were harvested annually within the county.

Record cold spells in the late decades of the century ruined some annual crops, though none damage to the groves was soon repaired. In 1989, weather reporting stations at Fellsmere and Vero Beach recorded lows of 23 degrees Fahrenheit. Some growers recorded temperatures even lower. Of the devastating February 1989 freeze, one farmer was quoted that "I started out to save my fruit. Then I tried to save my trees. I should have just saved my oil." The Florida Citrus Mutual reported that the northern coastal region of Indian River County, including Orchid Island, experienced the most damage that year. Occasional hurricanes struck the county, such as Hurricane David in 1979, which ripped the fruit from trees in Wabasso and elsewhere.

The county's cattle industry, still in its infancy at the close of World War II, matured in the 1950s. Popular magazines, such as *Collier's,* reminded the nation that "there were cattle in Florida before there were people in Texas," but joked about "pole and china" cattle in the South that were "so weak that they had to be propped up with a pine pole," and so "pore you could milk them with a china cup." Significant advances came from scientific research at the University of Florida that addressed mineral deficiencies in the soils of various types of pasturelands. By 1950, Florida ranked twelfth nationally in beef cattle production. Indian River County contained only a few large ranches. During the next decade,

The Indian River County cattle Industry grew significantly in the post-World War II era. This collection of buildings on 90th Avenue typifies the county's larger farms and ranches.

however, forest and wetlands yielded to pastures and the county's cattle industry became big business.

The Jo-Bar Dairy Farm of John and Barbara Tripson, organized about 1915 by Barbara's father, Waldo Sexton, grew into an agricultural showplace by mid-century. Hugh Corrigan, and his sons, Hugh Corrigan, Jr. and Pat Corrigan, organized the Corrigan Ranch, one of the county's premier beef ranches, in 1949. Located west of Vero Beach, the spread contained nearly 10,000 acres and 300 head of cattle. Specializing in Herefords, Pat Corrigan used a combined "JP" brand to mark his cattle. The Kromhout family also stocked Herefords on its Indian River County ranch. Natives of Holland, the Kromhouts used "polled cattle," that is, a breed of Hereford with a mound of bone on their heads, rather than horns. The Kromhouts began ranching in the 1950s and by 1961 maintained a herd of 200 cows on their White-Face Acres ranch. In addition to 14 pastures, the Kromhout farm contained 160 acres of citrus. The Holman family, dealers in automobiles since 1925 and operators of Vero Beach Airport Service, established Blue Cypress Lake Ranch in the 1940s. The area of Twenty-Mile Bend also contains ranches established in the late 1910's and early 1920's by Kenneth Prince, Latt Maxey, and the Surrency family. Those ranches are still owned by decendents of the same families. Although on most ranches pedigree cattle began to replace scrub stock and "pole and china" cows, Fellsmere's Gilbert Barkowskie experimented with cross breeding purebred cattle and scrub cows. The resulting offspring displayed characteristics of early native stock with good bloodlines, suited to a variety of ranges and pastures. The Florida Cattlemen's Association recognized Barkowskie as one the state's earliest cowmen to perfect that breeding practice.

One national publication, the *American Magazine,* in an article entitled "Cow Hands on the Grape Fruit Range," called attention to the unusual combination of orange groves and cattle ranches on the same farms. As early as 1924, economist J. Russell Smith had predicted such a development. The Texas fever tick hampered growth of the cattle industry until 1944, when dipping vat programs finally eliminated the pests. After World War II, nutritious citrus pulp, open winter pastures, scientific experiments, and significant investments in land and livestock helped to promote the state's cattle industry. But new range laws changed the culture of cattle ranching. Prominent cowman Charlie Lykes observed sadly in 1952 that the "cracker cowpuncher" was disappearing, replaced by businessmen who remained indoors rather than on the range. At the close of the twentieth century, Indian River County supported nearly 60 cattle ranches and 20,000 cows. Indicative of the consolidation within the cattle industry, by 1997 fifteen thousand cows were herded on just eight of the county's ranches.

Located on 14th Avenue south of Nineteenth Place, Vero Beach's Masonic Lodge was among the few social halls constructed in Indian River County after World War II. The Lodge dedicated the building on February 23, 1950.

After a more than twenty-year hiatus, building construction in Indian River County resumed in the post-war years where it had left off when the Boom collapsed in 1926. Five Vero Beach religious denominations, the Baptist, Catholic, Community, Methodist, and Presbyterian congregations, built new churches between 1945 and 1965. Sebastian's Methodist congregation completed a new sanctuary in 1964. The City of Vero Beach constructed a new city hall, and county authorities added a new library and high school to the city. The Vero Lodge erected a meeting hall in 1950. More than 650 new houses went up between 1947 and 1952.

The promise of wealth through land development continued in the late twentieth century to attract investors to east central Florida, just as it had E. Nelson Fell and Herman J. Zeuch decades before. On the barrier island that early settlers called Orchid and east of Winter Beach and Gifford, developer Fred Tuerk started a 2,600-acre river-to-ocean development. The General Development Corporation undertook an ambitious project in Sebastian during the 1960s. After initiating a celebrated development in Naples, landscape architect H. Milton Link turned his attention to Florida's east coast to develop the Moorings property for the Lobo-Gonzales family. This exclusive development was located along U.S. A1A, south of Vero Beach. Nearby, Joseph Walton began the ocean-front community of Floralton Beach. Adjacent to Wabasso Beach, John Morrison built his investment company, in part, by developing seasonal homes at secluded "Summerplace." In the old Riomar section of the barrier Island, St. Edward's School, based on the model of St. Andrew's in Boca Raton, was established.

Sebastian's Dale Wimbrow reported on these and other activities in his *Indian River News,* earning him recognition from the Florida Press Association. A photographer for the U.S. Navy during construction of the Vero Beach Naval Air Station, Wimbrow later settled at Sebastian, which he characterized as "God's toadstool." He never sold the *Indian River News* because he believed that nobody

In 1952, Indian River County residents celebrated the designation of A1A as the Charles A. Mitchell Memorial Highway. A Vero Beach attorney and county prosecutor, Mitchell served in the Florida Legislature in 1931. The ceremony dedicating the highway convened at Alex MacWilliam Park. Posing next to the plaque are (from the left) Alfred McKetham, chairman of the State Road and Bridge Committee; Vero Beach mayor Alex MacWilliam; State Senator Merrill P. Barber; Jeanette MacWilliam; and Florida's Governor Fuller Warren.

else would be crazy enough "to lose money trying to tell the truth," his description of the newspaper business. In the 1960s, the *Vero Beach Press-Journal* consistently captured the Florida Press Association's awards for its coverage of local news and community service. John Justin Schumann, Jr., a graduate of Mercer University, took the family's newspaper heritage into its third generation. Near the close of the century, the paper's excellence drew the attention of several national publishing firms, including E. W. Scripps, Inc., which in the mid-1990s acquired the *Press-Journal,* affectionately known for decades by county residents as the "PJ."

City and county authorities established a number of new recreational areas and parks on the peninsula, including Jaycee Park, Round Island Park, South Beach Park, and Wabasso Beach Park. The State of Florida also created the Sebastian Inlet State Recreation Area on both sides of the Sebastian Inlet. Earlier parks within the city of Vero Beach were Humiston Park and MacWilliam Park, which honored the memories of beloved, long-time residents and community leaders Dr. W. H. Humiston and Alex MacWilliam. Charles Parks, Vero Beach's first director of recreation, helped steer the city's park development. Charles Park, located at the end of 15th Street, was dedicated to him following his tenure as director. Another park, within the McAnsh Park residential development, was named in honor of Troy E. Moody, Jr., who was killed in the Korean War.

A number of new organizations responded to an expanding demand for recreational and cultural satisfaction. A growing consciousness of the area's history reflected the advancing age of the county and its sense of place, spawning the development of the McLarty State Museum, Indian River County Historical Society Museum, Indian River County Citrus Museum, Sebastian Area Historical Museum, and the Sebastian Inlet Fishing Museum.

The landscape changed as fields of citrus and woodlands yielded to housing tracts and commercial strips. Residents in the Johns Island area incorporated Indian River Shores, a new municipal government. Developer Fred Tuerk helped drive the incorporation and served as mayor of the town. A newcomer to Indian River County in 1950, Tuerk acquired the Windswept Hotel and 3,000 acres of river-to-ocean real estate. From a fledgling town of 19 residents in 1960, the exclusive neighborhood blossomed to a population of 2,500 in the mid-1990s. The Town of Orchid grew hardly at all. Organized in the late 1960s, it claimed only 21 residents three decades later. The Orchid Island, Orchid Isle Estates, and Johns Island developments introduced into the county high-end exclusive communities in the 1970s and 1980s. Although the completion of Florida's Turnpike and Interstate 95 funneled visitors away from the traditional eastern routes through the county, a rising tide of motorists more than compensated for the loss. Condominiums and a novel use of those housing units for recreational purposes, the so-called timeshare, contributed to the county's resort and vacation image. During the closing decade of the twentieth century, "superstores" and "mega-malls" appeared along S.R. 60, redirecting growth west of the oldest settled parts of the county and placing new pressures on commercial interests in the established downtowns to maintain their businesses.

Among the victims of change were many of the old and historic buildings within the county, demolished to make way for replacement structures or left simply to decay. New buildings replaced two classic icons of the 1920s, the Hotel Vero Del Mar and Royal Park Inn. Picturesque schools in Vero Beach fell to bulldozers and wrecking balls. Some who helped destroy the old school buildings marveled at their sturdy construction. New buildings added along U.S. 1 in Sebastian and downtown Vero Beach compromised the character of the county's oldest cities. The county seat improved its cultural and government services with the construction of a new courthouse and library in the 1990s, but at the cost of some of its small-town ambiance.

Fortunately, much of the tangible heritage was preserved. Fruit packing operations continue at several old and weathered citrus houses. The downtowns and older neighborhoods of Sebastian and Vero Beach retained their 1920s ambiance in places, thanks in great part to organizers and dedicated volunteers of the Indian River County Historical Society and later the St. Sebastian River Area Historical Society. A native of Pennsylvania, Walter "Wally" Skiscim had been stationed at the Vero Beach Naval Air Station during WWII. He returned to Vero Beach in 1946 and began to document some of the county's older buildings on the eve of their destruction. Skiscim also painstakingly prepared photographs of buildings that had appeared in decades-old issues of the *Vero Beach Press-Journal,* helping to build the archives of the Indian River County Historical Society. One visionary businessman, Robert L. Brackett, carefully rehabilitated three historic buildings in Vero Beach: the Vero Theater, the Pueblo Arcade, and

Vero Beach's Methodists organized in April 1914, and completed a wood-frame sanctuary three years later. A new sanctuary was completed on Twentieth Street in 1951, one of many changes as the county matured in the late-20th century. The wood-frame church survived until December 1967, when it burned in a spectacular fire.

the Indian River County Courthouse. Sand streets shaded by old-growth oak canopies continued to cast their shade over Riomar's historic section. Rehabilitated historic school buildings in Fellsmere, Wabasso, and Winter Beach remained in use, their original appearance largely intact. The Marian Fell Library in Fellsmere, the St. Sebastian River Area Woman's Club, and the Vero Beach Woman's Club continued to serve those communities within historic buildings.

The national historic preservation movement charts its active beginnings to Congressional approval of the National Historic Preservation Act of 1966. Quickly thereafter, efforts began in Indian River County to identify and then to preserve historic sites. The federally-protected Pelican Island National Wildlife Refuge was listed in the National Register of Historic Places in 1966. The nearby Spanish Fleet Survivors & Salvors Camp Site followed in 1970. In the 1980s, some residents took deliberate steps to preserve the county's tangible heritage. The imminent destruction in the early 1980s of the 1903 Vero Beach Florida East Coast Railway Station aroused preservation efforts by a newly formed organization, the Indian River County Historical Society. Led by Hazel Crews, its president, the Society acquired the building from the FEC, moved it to a new site, began its rehabilitation, and in 1987 obtained listing of the historic depot in the

National Register of Historic Places. It was the first building in Indian River county to achieve such designation. At its new site, about one-half mile north of the original location, the depot was carefully adapted for use as a museum and office. Between 1990 and 1999 sixteen additional buildings in Fellsmere, Sebastian, and Vero Beach were added to the National Register of Historic Places.

The residents in the north county sought help in establishing their own local Sebastian Area Historical Society. The committee formed by the Indian River County Historical Society to save the old community building in Pocahontas Park became a new preservation group named the Vero Heritage, Inc. Under the leadership of Millie Bunnell, the building was successfully saved and renamed the Heritage Center. The Fellsmere's Beautification Committee was established to save the 1916 Fellsmere School and other buildings along Fellsmere's main street. One of the most significant challenges of the Society occurred between 1983 and 1986 when the historic and scenic county road along the Indian River Lagoon was threatened by developers. This seven-mile public road called Jungle Trail was saved and in 1995 designated by the State of Florida as the Jungle Trail Greenway. The Society in the Gifford Community undertook relocation of a black church. Established by laborers on Henry Flagler's FEC railroad in the Sebastian area, the 1908 Macedonia Church was moved to the predominately black Gifford Community to be restored and opened as a black history museum. Between 1989 and 1999, the society obtained grants to complete surveys of historic properties in the unincorporated area of the county, as well as in Fellsmere, Sebastian and Vero Beach. An archaeological survey of the entire county was also conducted and, in the same decade, sixteen additional properties were added to the National Register.

The growing fascination with the heritage and history of Indian River County precipitated other types of activities. Oral history interviews conducted from the 1960s to the 1980s recorded the memories of many long-time residents, including Merrill P. Barber, Purnell Kennedy, "Doc" Charlie McClure, John J. Schumann, Sr., Earle G. Thatcher, and James T. Vocelle, Sr. The *Vero Beach Press-Journal*, the oldest newspaper in the county, published periodic award-winning editions that recaptured the region's rich past. Published works appeared in the 1950s. Anna Pearl Leonard Newman offered an early glimpse of local activities with *Early Life on the Indian River*. Vero Beach's Methodist congregation prepared its own chronicle, *Ours, A Godly Heritage: A History of The First Methodist Church, Vero Beach, Florida; 1914-1954*. The First Baptist Church of Vero Beach followed in 1965 with a special anniversary edition of *Church Chimes,* which recounted that congregation's history. A councilman of Vero Beach, J. Noble Richards, compiled and privately published in 1968 *Florida's Hibiscus City: Vero Beach.* As a part of its contribution to the celebration of America's 200th birthday celebration in 1976, the Indian River County's Action '76 Bicentennial Committee published Charlotte Lockwood's *Florida's Historic Indian River County,* filled with photographs. The Indian River County Historical Society coordinated the efforts of Kathy Pickel to write a student's history of the county called *Changes,* a publication used by fourth grade students. Local societies began to publish historical accounts. Two volumes, *Tales of Sebastian* (1990) and *More Tales of Sebastian* (1992), issued by the St. Sebastian River Area Historical Society, treat the history of the county's oldest continuously-occupied regions. The process of recognizing Indian River County's contribution to Florida's history in the last quarter century has gained significance itself, for in these activities the county's residents and visitors can better recognize Indian River County's sense of place. In observance of those achievements and the county's 75th anniversary, the Indian River County Historical Society initiated publication of this volume.

Such activities resulted from the sense of loss that many citizens experienced as they witnessed the rapid changes of the late twentieth century. As the century wore on, people throughout the nation, especially in Florida, one of the nation's fastest growing states in the second half of the twentieth century, developed growing concerns about the natural and built environments around them. The factors that first attracted people to Indian River County in the early twentieth century — a rural agricultural heritage, small close-knit towns and villages, and a distinctive sense of place — were preserved despite the threats. At century's end, the citizens of Indian River County had the luxury knowing they had acted in a responsible way to deal with the challenges of inevitable growth, refusing to accept the virtual wall-to-wall, northward-creeping development that characterized most of southeast Florida. The issues of growth and change and quality of life promise the greatest challenges in the new century. But if, as the future unfolds, the residents of Indian River County reaffirm the county's "sense of place," they will successfully deal with those challenges.

Additional Readings

A variety of primary and secondary source materials was consulted in gathering information for this book. They included public documents, official records, newspapers, interviews, manuscripts, and published books and articles.

Legal instruments at Brevard County Courthouse in Titusville, Indian River County Courthouse in Vero Beach, and St. Lucie County Courthouse in Fort Pierce hold a wealth of information about the region's landholders and residents. Minute books compiled by school boards in Brevard, Indian River, and St. Lucie Counties and minutes books held at Fellsmere City Hall and Vero Beach City Hall provide important details about early decisions and events.

Reference and source materials are on file at the Main Library of Indian River County at Vero Beach and the Marian Fell Library in Fellsmere. Back issues of the *Vero Beach Press-Journal,* its predecessors, and the *Fellsmere Farmer* and *Fellsmere Tribune* offer important intelligence about personalities, events, and development. Extensive vertical files and interviews yield newspaper clippings, postal service documents, and the memories of early settlers. The Indian River County Historical Society holds the best collection of photographs depicting the county's history. A distant second best is the collection at the Florida State Photographic Archives in Tallahassee.

Several local histories are available. Anna Newman's *Early Life on the Indian River* was one of the earliest of those, released in the 1950s. In 1968, attorney J. Noble Richards published the *Florida's Hibiscus City: Vero Beach.* Charlotte Lockwood provided the first countywide history in 1976 with *Florida's Historic Indian River County.* More recently, *Tales of Sebastian* (1990) and *More Tales of Sebastian* (1992) contain vignettes of that community's heritage. The *Florida Historical Quarterly* contains a number of articles devoted to Indian River County topics, including articles by Gordon Patterson on E. Nelson Fell and the sugar industry that the journal published in 1997.

Historical and architectural descriptions of buildings listed in the National Register of Historic Places can be found in the National Register files at the Florida Department of State, Division of Historical Resources, in Tallahassee. The same division holds numerous archaeological reports, compiled in association with on-going investigations. Dr. Eugene Lyon's superb treatment of the early settlement of Florida, *The Enterprise of Florida: Pedro Menéndez de Avilés and the Spanish Conquest of 1565-1568* remains the definitive account of a period in which events in what is now Indian River County played a surprisingly significant part.

Illustration Credits

Illustrations on pages 5, 6 and 9 are courtesy of the Florida Photographic Archives, Florida Department of State. The remaining illustrations, including maps and photographs, are from the private collections of County Historian Ruth Stanbridge, Sidney Johnston, Historic Property Associates, and, primarily, the Indian River County Historical Society.